The Chase for
Beauty

The Chase for
Beauty

Robert Mendelson

New York

The Chase for Beauty

By Robert Mendelson

© 2007 All rights reserved.

ISBN: 978-1-60037-278-0 (Hardcover)
ISBN: 978-1-60037-277-3 (Paperback)

Published by:

MORGAN · JAMES
THE ENTREPRENEURIAL PUBLISHER
www.morganjamespublishing.com

Morgan James Publishing, LLC
1225 Franklin Ave. Suite 325
Garden City, NY 11530-1693
800.485.4943
www.MorganJamesPublishing.com

Cover & Interior Design by:
Megan Johnson
Johnson2Design
www.Johnson2Design.com
megan@Johnson2Design.com

Habitat
for Humanity®
Peninsula
Building Partner

Acknowledgments

Until I considered writing this book, I hadn't met Dr. Dennis Hurwitz, even though we lived in the same Pittsburgh neighborhood for several years. I certainly knew him through newspaper headlines, though. His life seemed to have more drama than an action-packed novel. I always thought to myself he had quite a story to tell.

When we finally did meet, it was in his home, hours after dinnertime. I got there on time, but he wasn't there yet, so I chatted with his wife, Linda, until he arrived after his 12-hour workday at the hospital (a typical day for him, I would later learn). He hadn't eaten yet, so we adjourned to the dining room where Linda served him a reheated full-course dinner that would make most restaurants proud. He ate with gusto while I explained to him why I thought his life would make a fascinating story and he, in turn, told me why he thought his life would make a fascinating story. By dessert, we both decided to move forward. I would have complete creative control, and he would open his life to me.

For the next year, I conducted around 100 interviews to capture what both of us envisioned during our first meeting. What follows is a story about love, about triumphs, about tragedy. More than that, it is a story about perseverance and about having faith that the world isn't inherently ugly. It's a story that I don't think can be told too much.

I wish to thank Dr. Hurwitz, his wife, Linda, and the rest of his family for their candor during my interviews. I wish to thank also the many others who willingly shared how their lives intertwined with Dr. Hurwitz, whether those moments stemmed from joyous, troubling, or tragic circumstances.

Like all writers, I owe a debt of gratitude to my own family, too, for their support and their love. Thank you to my wife, Debra, and to my teenage children, Lauren and Jesse.

Lastly, I would be remiss in not mentioning that this special story might never have been told had David Hancock, the founder of Morgan James Publishing, not grasped the relevance of Dr. Hurwitz's life and times. All of us look for heroes everywhere—in sports, in Hollywood, on magazine covers. What we fail to realize is that sometimes heroes live in our own neighborhoods.

Chapter One

D r. Dennis Hurwitz freely admits that he doesn't consider himself a handsome man. In truth, he probably isn't, at least not by Hollywood standards, though many of his family members, friends, patients, even strangers would disagree, especially when they take into account his age. In a life that spans nearly six decades, he has a full head of hair that shows no signs of succumbing to middle age, a trim waist line that could compete with an athletic college student, and, perhaps most important, a youthful level of energy and perpetual air of self confidence that affect his appearance far beyond his physical features.

While more than a few baby boomers might be envious of his youthful persona, it is probably fortunate for him that he can perceive flaws in his features. In a way, it is a job requirement. Dr. Hurwitz is a plastic surgeon, which means his livelihood depends on the premise of imperfection.

As he walks, just before dawn, along a sidewalk bordering the Chicago River in downtown Chicago, Dr. Hurwitz, attired in a business suit, isn't dwelling on his imperfections. There is no time to do so. He has just finished a live 5:50 AM morning show interview at WLS-TV 7, Chicago's ABC television affiliate, and, before most business executives have their second cup of coffee, he will complete another interview down river with another local morning show on Fox's WFLD-TV 32.

He is in demand by the media. A few months ago, May 2005, marked the release of his book, *Total Body Lift* (New York: MDPublish.com). The Total Body Lift is his remedy for what has become a more common condition, especially among the obese who have undergone the increasingly popular bariatric surgery that shrinks the stomach. For many individuals, their significant weight loss leaves behind vast amounts of sagging, excess skin, which neither exercise nor diet will reduce. Dr. Hurwitz's surgical solution, extensively detailed in his 192-page book, is the Total Body Lift, which is described on the book's cover as a *reshaping of the breasts, chest, arms, thighs, hips, back, waist, abdomen, and knees.*

What makes his solution noteworthy isn't so much his reshaping recommendation; it is doing a Total Body Lift in a single procedure for otherwise healthy patients, an operation that can last nearly half a day and leave a patient with more than 2,000 stitches. Dr. Hurwitz notes in his book that *my surgeon detractors admonish that 10-hour elective reconstructive operations are an expression of exuberance, perhaps testosterone excess,* but he counters that objection by stating a *synergism* takes place in the operating room that can lead to better cosmetic results and only one recovery time for the patient.

The book has received strong support from several professionals in the medical community, including Dr. Walter J. Pories, who is widely regarded as one of the founders of bariatric surgery. Dr. Pories, the professor of surgery and biochemistry in the Brody School of Medicine at East Carolina University and past president of the American Society for Bariatric Surgery, agreed to write the book's foreword, where he praised *the remarkable contributions of Dr. Hurwitz who has now taught us that the body can be reshaped in its entirety and that our own bariatric surgical patients can return to a life with a full cup. For the morbidly obese, he has produced the second miracle. I strongly recommend this book to anyone who deals with bariatric surgical patients not only to become familiar with the possible, but also to celebrate a great story of success.*

Two book reviews posted on Amazon.com share Dr. Pories enthusiasm:

A Reconstruction Miracle

(book grade: four out of five stars)

If anyone can restore the human form as close to God created, it is Dr. Hurwitz. His dedication to this area of reconstructive surgery is com-

mendable. I am so convinced of his expertise that I will be meeting him myself next month. This book has given me hope, and I thank him for this. The book was a clear cut, easy-to-follow explanation of this procedure. Case-by-case photos were included to see his work in living color. I recommend this book to anyone considering this surgery.

Margaret, Florida

July 10, 2005

Total Body Lift—The Ultimate Transformation of Body and Spirit

(book grade: four out of five stars)

As a member of Dr. Hurwitz's international clientele, I believe this book can absolutely transform your life! Formerly obese, I faced the common problem of massive extra sheets of hanging skin after losing the weight—was there a way to fix this? His innovative Total Body Lift, done all at once, reassures us this is possible; it can help us regain self-confidence and our place in the world. Throughout are valuable first-hand patient insights from their awesome journeys discovering their 'authentic selves'—re-entering the world with optimism and joy. I just wish I had found Dr. Hurwitz's solution many years ago. As Oliver Wendell Holmes said, "A moment's insight is sometimes worth a life's experience."

Martha, Canada

June 29, 2005

Dr. Hurwitz spent more than a year of weekends and evenings writing *Total Body Lift* for an audience beyond bariatric patients and the medical community. As he stated in the introduction, he also wrote *Total Body Lift* for readers who might be *interested to get inside the head of a busy, innovative plastic surgeon.* He seems to be as proud of the book as he is of the before and after photos of his Total Body Lift patients.

The publishing news isn't all good, though. There have been no reviews, good or bad, from the national news media. It's not on any best-seller lists, either. "Book sales are pathetic," he admits. "I would starve as a writer. I'm thrilled that I wrote it, and I have it as an educational, marketing tool for my patient population. I am not so sure with the dollars I have spent on marketing, $50,000 more or less, that it has been anywhere close to bringing the book sales."

Giving the book every chance to succeed is partly what motivated him to be a guest on the morning talk shows. In between the live broadcasts, he walks back to his hotel, the Sheraton Chicago Hotel and Towers, where he will have a complimentary continental breakfast served in the hotel's restaurant. While eating a bowl of cereal and a bagel, he glances at *USA Today* and mingles with his medical colleagues, who are also in Chicago. Plastic surgeons from across the country are there for the annual scientific meeting of the Plastic Surgery Educational Foundation, the American Society of Maxillofacial Surgeons, and the American Society of Plastic Surgeons, a society that bills itself as *the largest plastic surgery specialty organization in the world.* The five-day meeting is advertised to *ensure board-certified plastic surgeons continue to offer patients the latest techniques, technologies, and trends in both cosmetic and reconstructive plastic surgery.*

However, Dr. Hurwitz won't be one of the keynote speakers to the nearly 5,000 doctors, medical personnel, and exhibitors in attendance. "I was disappointed not to be asked to present my work in the large open-session panel," he says. Most of the doctors attend those open sessions. He did take solace in being invited by the ASPS special course committee to give a one-hour lecture on breast reshaping after massive weight loss, which is part of his Total Body Lift. The crowd there would be around 100 doctors.

Dr. Scott Spear, chief of plastic surgery, Georgetown University Hospital, and president of the ASPS, explains why Dr. Hurwitz wasn't asked to present his work before the larger audience: "I think that the body surgery field is in its infancy in many ways. It is still sorting itself out. Exactly how it sorts itself out remains to be seen. I think Dennis is clearly one of the leaders at the moment in terms of coming up with ideas and showing what he does. Like any new field, you can take the telecom industry for example, there is a lot of shakeup that goes on. Exactly what shakes out, I don't think has been sorted out yet. I think it is going to take a few years to come up with the best pathways, the safest pathways, the ones that are the most reliable."

The speaking invitation omission to the open session doesn't seem to overly faze Dr. Hurwitz; it certainly doesn't slow him down. After breakfast, he'll find the time to dash upstairs to his hotel room before his next interview. Sitting on the foot of the bed, he'll make multiple cell phone calls, first to his New York City publicist, and then to patients who he thinks might want to tell their story in a television studio. The calls help solidify upcoming appearances on NBC's *Today* and the nationally syndicated *Inside Edition.*

During that pre-dawn riverside walk on a brisk, autumn morning, a walk that took him from the ABC television studio to the Sheraton Hotel, he could have contemplated the peacefulness of the moment, perhaps even where life had taken him. From the concrete banks along the Chicago River, Dr. Hurwitz could embrace an odd combination of capitalism and nature—the tranquility of Lake Michigan, one of the five Great Lakes, was at the approachable eastern horizon, while within his sight in every other direction was Chicago's massive skyline that houses some of the world's leading corporations, cultural institutions, and retail establishments. The rising sun seemed to put a hazy spotlight on the poetic convergence that on this day included Dr. Hurwitz.

It was one of those moments of beauty that exceeded adjectives, a gift from the heavens for self-reflection, precisely the kind of gift that Dr. Hurwitz tries to avoid. "I don't want time alone," he willingly admits.

Invariably, time alone for him doesn't evoke thoughts about what he has accomplished, what he has done right, what he has to be thankful for. Instead, any time alone too often brings back his loss, his horror, his realization that what might have been can never be. Fortunately for him,

Chapter One

the chance for his pain to surface once again on this picturesque morning disappears as fast as it came. The sun continued its rise, turning the spotlight into daylight; then the Sheraton Hotel suddenly dwarfed his view, and the hotel's continental breakfast was now being served. Like every other morning, Dr. Hurwitz overpowered what could have been paralyzing reflections. He knows he can't be a man of reflection, a man who continually wonders, "What if that hadn't happened?" To survive, to be a great doctor, to be a loving husband, to be a wonderful father, he knows he has to be a man who moves forward.

His drive is not lost on his colleagues. "I don't think Dennis is typical of surgeons in general," says Dr. Spear. "I would have to put Dennis in the top five or ten percent of surgeons in terms of their level of energy and their desire to excel or to be recognized. Dennis has particularly high expectations. Ninety percent of surgeons are just happy to do their surgery, go home, and play with their kids. I don't think they all want to be superstars. Not at all. Dennis represents the smaller group."

Dr. Hurwitz agrees without a hint of pride or remorse. "It's all true," he says simply as he recalls a pledge he made to himself early in his medical career: "When I walk though the halls, people are going to know who I am." This drive to excel, to keep moving forward, not only defines his life; it has, in all likelihood, saved his life, at least until now.

In the makeup room at the Fox studio, Dr. Hurwitz seems at ease. Not much makeup is needed, because he already had foundation applied to him at his earlier interview. All he needs is some brushing of the hair, a bit of hair spray, and he is ready for the airwaves once again. If he is nervous, there are no noticeable signs.

On the set, a producer tells him he will be situated behind a desk, standing with his interviewer, Tamron Hall, a very attractive co-anchor for *Fox News in the Morning*. The other co-anchor, Patrick Elwood, will introduce the segment. This is live television, so there is no "Take One," It's just action:

"The popularity of cosmetic surgery is skyrocketing, and, now, a new surgery claims to reshape your entire body," says Mr. Elwood. "Tamron is learning more with the plastic surgeon who created what is called the Total Body Lift. Tamron——"

The red light atop the camera focused on Dr. Hurwitz and co-anchor Hall is suddenly illuminated. Dr. Hurwitz still seems relaxed, his hands resting on the desk while the cover of his book is reflected in the background between the two of them.

"Very interesting, Patrick; I am here with Dr. Dennis Hurwitz from the University of Pittsburgh, and he is getting international attention for the surgery that he has created, Total Body Lift. It is designed for patients who have lost massive amounts of weight but are left with that flabby skin. We're looking at this video [a video shows a woman whose arm is held up by Dr. Hurwitz, which reveals excessive amounts of sagging skin hanging below her bicep]. Take a look at that. Now some of the patients are even moms who want to tighten their tummies after having a baby, and he wrote a book about this revolutionary surgery; it's called *Total Body Lift* [the book cover appears on the television screen], and Dr. Hurwitz is with us now. Thank you so much for joining us. [The camera returns its focus on Dr. Hurwitz and Ms. Hall.]

"Good morning," are Dr. Hurwitz's first words.

"This is fascinating. You actually performed this surgery on I believe 70 patients?"

"Yes I have. We started this innovation about three years ago, and there have been 70 patients, going on more; we're very interested in getting the body totally remade in one stage or maybe two."

"Now you're the surgeon who is bringing this to the country. I mean no one else is doing this, you are the person who invented it, which is fascinating to me, because how do you develop a new form of surgery?"

"Well, my book talks about that. It's complex, but we, dissatisfied with what's already out there, take incremental steps of adjustments and, over a two- or three-year period, it leads to a point where we have the courage to really move forward."

"Now is it the same as when you do a facelift? I mean the concept behind facelifts is to tighten, you know, wrinkles or whatever. Is it the same thing with the body?"

"A body lift is a similar concept, because gravity does have the same role. We have to take out skin and move what is remaining in an artistic way and put scars where they are least visible, under underwear or in the brassiere, so that somebody can wear skimpy clothing and not be too noticeable."

"Well, let's take a look at some of the pictures, before and after pictures [before and after photos of a woman's torso are shown]. This first picture is a woman who had the Total Body Lift in her abdominal area. Describe what we see that is different there, doctor."

"You can see overhanging her panties a loose skin that really goes all the way up to her shoulders and down her thighs, and the panty line covers the scars that resulted after tightening her skin and making a whole new belly button."

"How much weight do you recall this person lost?"

"She lost 120 pounds by exercise and diet, quite a courageous 20-year-old woman."

"Absolutely! Let's take a look at another picture. This is another example. [Before and after photos of another woman's torso—the before photo shows two mammoth rolls of fat, almost like a second set of breasts just above a huge pot belly; the after photo has no rolls, just a contoured body with a visible scar at the panty line.] Wow!"

"This woman lost 200 pounds and still looked like the *before* and this [the after photo] is the front view; you can see her belly button on the outside there, and the scar lies around where the panty would be, and that's part of a 10-hour operation."

"Now, are you cutting and removing skin, taking it off the patient completely?"

"Absolutely; in her case 18 pounds of skin and fat were removed."

"Amazing! Let's take another, because these pictures are incredible; I want you to see them all. Arm reduction, there is a before and after picture of an arm reduction. [Before and after photos are shown of a woman with sagging skin under the arm—the before photo is like a second arm dangling under her bicep; the after photo shows a toned arm, with a fine, straight scar visible underneath the arm.] Now a lot of women complain about that, that flabby skin under the arm."

"It is a woman's problem, even if you haven't lost a lot of weight, with aging, and putting a scar very discreetly on the inner aspect of the arm, shaping the arm nicely, works out very nicely when the problem is this severe. [The camera returns to host and guest.]"

"Now this surgery will cost you about $50,000. Is it something that's covered usually by insurance, because I know that a number of gastric bypass patients have that extra skin and need those Total Body Lifts. Is it usually covered by insurance?"

"No. Insurance may have a role to play for parts of the surgery, where the skin is being infected or irritated, but it plays a small role in what we call elective surgery. Now, it's very functional, and people are rehabilitated and live a better life because of the Total Body Lift, and it has an exhilarating experience for me to contribute to their life's improvement."

"Let's take a look at one more picture here [before and after photos of a male torso—the before photo shows a man with sizable breasts and skin hanging over his underwear; the after photo shows a well-proportioned male body with no signs of fat and one visible side scar, starting from the nipple and sweeping under the armpit]. This is a male patient, Justin, before and after. He is 22 years old. He went from 450 to 250 pounds after gastric bypass."

"I'm so glad you showed this picture, because this happens to men, too; they actually form breasts, and I have a new technique to more aesthetically remove that tissue and the abdomen all at one time. His operation was about nine hours, and he is a young politician in the Pittsburgh area and very happy with it. [The camera returns to Dr. Hurwitz and Ms. Hall.]"

"Now you were recently named one of America's top doctors, and you're teaching, or hope to be teaching, other doctors this procedure so that people don't have to travel to have this procedure done."

"I'm part of the residency program at the University of Pittsburgh, and my graduates are learning this, but I'm also receiving doctors from around the world, because this is new and different, and they need to learn to do it the right way."

"So, if someone is interested in having this done now, they would have to go directly to you?"

"Well, I am certainly the originator, and I have vast experience, and I am happy if they would like to contact me through my Web site or telephone and find out more."

"All right, well, if you want more information on Dr. Hurwitz and his Total Body Lift surgery, you can check out his Web site, which he mentioned, which is totalbodyliftsurgery.com. Very interesting, thank you so much for joining us."

"My pleasure, thank you very much, Tamron."

"Pat, back over to you. [The camera returns to Mr. Elwood.]"

The interview took five minutes. The time is 8:48 AM, and Dr. Hurwitz twice has been highly visible in the country's third largest television market. One of the Fox producers congratulates Dr. Hurwitz on a job well done. She marveled at his ability to speak in articulate sound bites. She would have been further impressed if she knew that he was functioning on less than five hours of sleep. The night before, he treated a dozen or so of his former residents to dinner, costing him around $500, and he didn't return to his hotel until after midnight. Had the producer actually known him, though, his performance in front of the camera, sleep or no sleep, wouldn't have been such a surprise. The interviews are an ideal outlet for him to interweave his ambition, his confidence, his medical prowess, and his charisma.

Throughout the day, his colleagues at the meeting seek him out to tell him that they saw him on television, some while rising from bed, others while working out in the hotel exercise room, and some more while having breakfast. All compliment him for his media savvy. If he has any detractors, they don't take the opportunity to tell him so face-to-face, at least not on this day.

He does have detractors, though. First and foremost is one of his former mentors and colleagues, Dr. Betty Jane McWilliams. She was director of the University of Pittsburgh's Cleft Palate Craniofacial Center, one of the largest centers of its type in the world, when Dr. Hurwitz fulfilled his plastic surgery residency there from 1975-1977 and subsequently became a member of the center's staff for some 20 years afterward.

"He is a good plastic surgeon," says Dr. McWilliams, who is now retired. After giving that preface, she is adamantly opposed to the way he conducts his private practice in terms of marketing. "Oh my goodness, it is advertising. He will get on any TV show or anything like that. I just wish he wouldn't do that. He is better than that. I think it is bad for him and bad for his profession."

Her distaste for marketing stems from the lack of protocol. "There is no peer review. There is no method of controlling it. Anybody can call off a telephone number and go and consult that person. People do it that way. They don't know how to investigate the reality of it. I think it is a bad approach to medicine, to law, anything." She believes patients should choose a doctor "based on reputation," not on advertisements or media exposure.

For the pre-baby boomers, the words of Dr. McWilliams, who grew up in during the Depression, must sound very familiar. However, in the *Bulletin of the American College of Surgeons,* a different outlook is proposed. The *Bulletin* is the monthly magazine for the college, which is proclaimed to be *a scientific and educational association of surgeons that was found-*

ed in 1913 to improve the quality of care for the surgical patient by setting high standards for surgical education and practice. Its 64,000 members, who are referred to as fellows, receive The *Bulletin*. In the magazine's upcoming January 2006 edition there will be a two-page column, titled *From My Perspective*, in which the college's executive director, Dr. Thomas R. Russell, will write:

This organization has always been fairly discreet about its accomplishments, refraining from activities that smack of self-promotion. In the past this sort of quiet modesty was admirable and helped the College maintain a highly professional image....

Many of us believe that the time has come for the College to reinstitute a public relations program—and to take a more aggressive and visible approach than we have used in the past. Some suggestions for improving the College's public visibility that we've received include hiring a public relations firm, developing an advertising program, and working with a publicist....As another means of communicating with the public, efforts are under way to develop and publish a book that explains the surgical experience and what is involved in having an operation in a way that the general population can understand....

It is time to break the mold of quiet modesty and let people know who we are, what we do, and what we stand for....

Dr. Hurwitz broke the mold several years ago, because he is not a man who waits for change; he initiates change. His boldness surely emanates from his self-confidence that, after proper deliberations, he will do the right thing. Potential consequences certainly don't inhibit him, which is impressive from a purely resilience standpoint, considering he has faced consequences that could have crushed him both professionally and personally.

As the sun sets in Chicago for the day, Dr. Hurwitz greets the one person who can make him think about consequences, a person who isn't afraid to tell him what he has done well, what he has done poorly, and what he should do in the future. Dr. Hurwitz doesn't always agree with Linda Hurwitz, but he always respects what she has to say, which might explain why they appear to still be in love after 36 years of marriage.

Dr. Hurwitz considers his wife a beautiful woman. No one would disagree. Like her husband, the years have been kind to her appearance. Together, they are a beautiful couple. Together, they are loving parents. Together, they live in an elegant, cozy home in Pittsburgh, Pennsylvania. Together, they provide no outward clues about what they have endured.

Ms. Hurwitz arrived in Chicago the day before the scheduled dinner honoring Dr. Spear, who has become a friend to her and her husband. She also planned to attend a luncheon/workshop for the wives of plastic surgeons who work in their husbands' offices. The subject piqued her interest, because six months ago, she began doing administrative work at the Hurwitz Center for Plastic Surgery. It marks quite a career change. For the previous 17 years, she served as the director of the Holocaust Center of Greater Pittsburgh. She says she was ready to take a break from such intense work, and her husband jumped at the chance to "hire her." Not content to be a full-time homemaker, she said yes to his part-time offer.

She arrived in Chicago in the early afternoon, a day before the workshop and dinner for Dr. Spear. By the time her plane landed at Chicago's Midway Airport, her husband was immersed in the meeting at the McCormick Place convention center. She let him be, opting instead to take a cab to the hotel and then do some window shopping along the Magnificent Mile's famed Michigan Avenue. The Hurwitzes had been apart for two days, but delaying their reunion until that evening didn't seem so excruciating to them or all that unusual, considering the couple first met when the Beatles were the rage.

"August of '64, early August '64," recalls Dr. Hurwitz.

"August 17th," says Ms. Hurwitz.

Chapter Two

Home for the summer in Baltimore, between his freshman and sophomore years at the University of Maryland, Dennis Hurwitz hears from his roommate, Wally, who happened to belong to another fraternity. He wanted to go to the summer pledge party at Dennis's fraternity, Phi Sigma Delta. "It was really not right," says Dennis, "but I said, 'Okay.' He sort of crashed our party."

Wally brought along a blind date. Her name was Linda Furst. She had just broken up with Robby, her boyfriend of two years. A mutual friend thought they would make a nice couple and set them up. Linda wasn't quite 16 years old, having just finished her sophomore year in high school. She recalls Dennis had a date, too. "Actually," she says, "she was the editor in chief of the newspaper at my high school. She was a pretty young woman."

In Dennis's eyes, his date wasn't as pretty as the girl with Wally. He liked everything about her—her refreshing, youthful smile; her long chestnut-colored hair streaked with natural highlights from the sun; her soft-looking skin; her well-developed, youthful figure. She was one of the California girls the Beach Boys sang about, anchored in Baltimore.

Wally finally introduced Linda to Dennis. "I was smitten by this girl," he recalls. "So pretty. So nice. And I just hung around her."

Their dates seemed to disappear. "After a while, I said, 'I'm going to marry her.'"

"He did," Linda says. "The night he met me, he said, 'I'm going to marry you.' I was really flattered and sort of swept away by it. No one had ever said to me before that they were going to marry me."

She knew better than to take him seriously. Nevertheless, she was intrigued. "The fact that he came on so confidently and strongly really resonated with me in a positive way. He seemed like someone who I could learn from, who would pull me to another level, who was stimulating and interesting and not boring. I saw that in him right away.

"You were talking about the times when you didn't think that, as a woman, you were going to support yourself. Maybe be a teacher a couple of years and then stop and have kids, but I hadn't formulated all of those thoughts yet. I was just going into eleventh grade."

After the party, she went home and told her mother the news. "I met this college guy who said he was going to marry me."

Linda wasn't the only one who was stunned. She remembers her mother's response. "I shouldn't have let you go to this party. He is too old for you."

But she did let her go.

"Dennis came around the next day," Linda remembers, "and took me to the Beatles movie, *A Hard Day's Night*, that was our very first date. And he started calling me. He wouldn't quit after that."

"That just typifies how I do things," he says. "I try to be rational, but some of my decisions are based on feelings and emotions; then, I work hard in a rational way to bring it to fruition."

He worked very hard, starting with that first night. "She was like a mirage. I had a sense I was talking to someone who was a dream, and the only way to catch that dream was to marry her. I had never said anything like that to anyone else." He had plenty of opportunities to do so, having continual girlfriends that lasted from a few weeks to six months at a time, starting around the age of 15.

Linda seemed different to him than all the others. "She gave me a sense of calmness and belonging, of tranquility in an otherwise intense time of my life."

The Chase for Beauty

The time was particularly intense, originating from a career aptitude test Dennis had taken when he was beginning high school. Like most teenagers, he hadn't given much thought about what would be his profession as an adult. Neither had his older brother, Stephen, who was ready for college. Their mom would put an end to their nonchalance. She was very much driven, an interior decorator at a time when most women didn't have careers, and she wanted to make sure her sons were going to be successes. A career aptitude test, given in Washington, DC, would point them in the right direction, she reasoned, so she and her two boys drove to the testing site from Baltimore.

His mother couldn't have been more pleased with the results. Steve would be an attorney, while Dennis would be a doctor. "Frankly, I thought I wasn't smart enough," says Dennis. But he would try. He took high school and then college very seriously, even after he discovered the love of his life, Linda, who inconveniently was living in a different city once he returned to the University of Maryland in College Park, Maryland, for his junior year. Classes remained his top priority, but Linda wasn't far behind. He returned home to Baltimore, a 30-minute commute, whenever he could, usually every other weekend.

Everything went as planned for a while. He maintained his grades and Linda's love. The following spring, Dennis made what he thought was a logical decision. He told Linda he wanted her to date him exclusively. "I didn't think she would go away," he says.

Her reply came in a letter.

March 11, 1965

Dear Dennis,

I hope this will not embitter you or cause you to hate me. You say even realizing the "worst possible about me, you still want me." Also you exaggerate in saying there is no one to talk to, that you want me. I've told you many times I cannot carry such a responsibility, and that I didn't want to get involved with you, yet it seemed even when several times we both tried

to make decisions or ease our relationship it still grew and persisted. I think now some of this must be released in a manner which I would have liked to tell you in person but not seeing you for several weeks would be too long to drag this out. I think you realized it already, anyway. I do still like Robby very, very much, as I am realizing more and more. I guess we really have something going between us since we always go back together, I've liked you, too, but in a different way, I'm afraid, than you want me to. I still want you as a good friend, however, I realize you want our relationship to be more than that. It is not fair for you to think I can give you more, because I cannot.

I hope we will remain true friends. I think we can. Also I know you understand and realize this must be.

Yours,

Linda

"I didn't take it well," he says. He didn't collapse, either. There were other girls. College girls. "I tried to replace her, but it wasn't the same. They all paled in comparison."

Dennis's parents sensed their son was depressed; they bought him a yellow GTO convertible. "Not a bad consolation prize," says Linda. She found out about the new car when she saw Dennis with a couple of college girls pictured in the society column of Baltimore's *Jewish Times* newspaper.

"Hot cars get women," Dennis shrugs. But there was only one woman he wanted, and he didn't give up. Even then, he was a man who always moved forward.

Linda, on the other hand, had Robby. But, after the junior prom, he felt like a consolation prize, too. "Ambivalent" is the word she uses to describe the relationship.

Meanwhile, one of Dennis's friends began working at a Baskin-Robbins ice cream store located in a small shopping center at the corner of Linda's street. It just so happens that Linda likes ice cream. She would go there occasionally, Dennis learned. One early day in June, while Linda mulls over the ice cream flavors, a GTO convertible pulls into the parking lot. Linda has something else to mull over. Dennis asked her to go for a ride.

The ride didn't last too long.

"We pulled over and parked someplace and started talking again," says Linda. "He told me how hurt he had been, and how much he wanted to be back with me, and would I reconsider. It was like my life flashed before me. I knew that if I went back, that was probably it. I couldn't hurt him again. I felt so badly how hurt he had been. I guess I realized that I did want to be with him, and that was it."

As they pulled away, Linda was astonished when she heard the song playing on the radio:

Are you ready? sing the male backups.

Yes I'm ready! reply the female backups.

Then, music star Barbara Mason sings her pop music hit, *Yes I'm Ready*, from the summer of '65:

I don't even know how to love you
Just the way you want me to
But I'm ready, ready to learn, to learn
Yes, I'm ready, ready to learn, to learn
To fall in love, to fall in love, to fall in love with you.

I don't even know how to hold your hand
Just to make you understand

Chapter Two

But I'm ready, ready, to learn, to learn

Yes, I'm ready, ready to learn, to learn

To hold your hand, make you understand

To hold your hand right now.

I don't even know how to kiss your lips, kiss your lips

At a moment like this

But I'm going to learn how to do

All the things you want me to.

Are you ready?

Yes, I'm ready.

Are you ready?

Yes, I'm ready

To fall in love, to fall in love

To fall in love right now.

"After that," says Linda, "I never went out with anybody else again."

"All I could say," Dennis adds, "is that I couldn't conceive of seeing someone else. She was all I cared about."

During their senior years, Dennis in college and Linda in high school, Dennis continued the weekend commute as often as he could, still around twice a month. In addition to those "kissing and necking" weekends, another release for their passion came through letter writing, like the penned note Dennis wrote to Linda in October 1965:

Dear Linda,

I am dying to see you. Last night I was lying in bed and my body was shaking or tingling. So much energy was surging through me, I couldn't sleep. Jeff thought I was crazy. A case of love sickness like mine, he never saw before. Jeff told me to think of you as being right next to me, but I couldn't. I needed your slow breathing, your warm caress, the pressure of your body. I needed someone to whisper to and someone to tell me what I wanted to hear. I needed that soft, warm flesh that abounds your body. I needed that long hair to weave my fingers through. I needed to be engrossed in you. To see your eyes, wide open and tear-filled, closed and graceful as if in a pleasant dream. I needed to feel surrounded by you. I needed to feel you in my care, held by me, supported and guided by me. I needed to follow those sensuous curves. Above all, I needed that sincere, warm kiss penetrating through my lips that shakes my whole body and sends my heart fluttering. I needed that gentle but firm massage or that swift strong rhythmic movement that tears me apart. BUT YOU WERE NOT THERE. How was I to sleep? What else can I say in this letter? Anything else seems trite and insignificant. The thought of you won't leave me, for I won't let it go.

Please God, keep Linda, keep me, keep us. Amen.

Love,

Dennis

God had plenty in store for Dennis and Linda, but nothing too dramatic during the next few years. Linda graduated from high school and, in just three years, earned a BS from Towson State College, majoring in English, in preparation for being a middle school English teacher; Dennis, also in three years, earned his BS degree from the University of Maryland and enrolled in the university's medical school. And nearly five years af-

Chapter Two

ter they first met, on June 8, 1969, they uttered the vows, "For better or worse." Like most newlyweds, they seemed to be expecting the "better" but poised to overcome whatever the "worse" would be.

On their wedding night, Dennis joked with Linda about what he had just done. "I cannot believe I just signed a contract for the next 50 years of my life. I think you are going to have to earn tenure." Ten years, he decided, sounded like a reasonable amount of time. Linda laughed, agreeing to the probationary period. What could go wrong?

The day after each said, "I do," they left for England for a honeymoon that would precede Dennis's medical school externship at London Hospital. Neither Dennis nor Linda came from affluent families, so money was a concern on the trip. "We had our $5 daybook," says Linda. "For $5 a day we could rent rooms at people's places."

The newlyweds traveled around the countryside. Within the first week, their touring took them to Edinburgh, Scotland. After a day of seeing the sights, they checked into a bed and breakfast.

"It was run by some matrons," says Dennis. "We were sitting there having high tea with them. It is maybe 9 o'clock at night or 10 o'clock at night, and they are chatting about God knows what, nothing that interests me, that's for sure." He politely thanks the women for their hospitality and says to Linda, "I think it is time for bed."

She must not have heard him. "I say it again and Linda says, 'There is the bedroom, you go ahead and go to sleep.'"

"No, we are tired."

"No, I'm not. I'll be there. I'm talking."

Dennis goes to the room. Alone.

"I lie on the bed, and I look at the ceiling trying to figure out how this woman can be so dense to not realize I wanted her to go to bed with me and that she is defying me. I am reflecting how my father would deal with this. I don't think he would put up with this shit. She knew what I wanted, and she openly defied me in front of other people I didn't even know for a reason that made no sense to me. It was quite clear, obviously, I had made a mistake, and we shouldn't be married."

It wasn't so clear to Linda; at least not until she came to the room.

"It took forever for her to get back to the room," says Dennis. "I said, 'Where have you been? Were you still talking to those old biddies out there?'"

"Yeah; they're so sweet, and I had to be nice to them. Why? What's the problem?"

"I wanted you here, and I wanted you here long ago."

"What, I have a curfew? I got married to get away from a curfew!"

Dennis laughed, but he was still angry. "We didn't have sex that night," he clearly remembers. "By the next day, I was all right. I really had the sense that a man controls a marriage. Do you know what happened? She changed my whole idea of a marital relationship in one night. I had unconsciously thought that I really had the final word on whatever is going to happen in this marriage. Any decisions.

"No longer."

Given the context of the time, 1969, the realization was profound for the man who joked that his wife needed to secure marital tenure. Women's Lib was just beginning for the country and for Dennis and Linda. But not for Shimon.

Chapter Two

The Chase for Beauty

Chapter Three

Growing up, Dennis shared a bedroom with his older brother, Shimon. Except, at the time, his name wasn't Shimon. It was Stephen. Like most younger brothers, Dennis looked up to his older brother. He fought with him, he played with him, and though he probably wouldn't admit it if asked by any adults, he loved him, too.

There were two other Hurwitz children, Bill and, the baby, Marilyn. Three years separated each child. For whatever reason, Bill says the two older ones and two younger ones paired off: "Dennis and Shimon were very tight. There was a gap there for Marilyn and me. That is the way that our family dynamics worked."

Stephen became Shimon when he was 30, after a trip to Israel that never ended. Until then, he remembers nothing dramatic in his life or in his Baltimore childhood shared with his brothers or sister. They were a stereotypical middle-class Jewish family that Shimon says led to a "very prosaic and mannered childhood."

The Hurwitz children might have been prosaic, but the parents were not. Shimon explains his parents' personalities though his siblings: "Denny and Bill inherited from my mother a very, what I would call, passionate, even-tempered, easygoing, somewhat aloof nature; they never got worked up about things. They were calm and collected. Whereas my sister and I are much more like my father, much more emotional, more volatile."

The divergent personalities didn't cause problems for the children, but it did for the parents. Marilyn bluntly says, "My parents fought like cats and dogs." For them, Bill says, it was a case of opposites no longer having an attraction for each other. "My dad was definitely mostly verbal. He liked to yell, a low threshold of patience. No concept of 'going with the punches' or anything like that. If you didn't do what he felt was right, he would start yelling. So we had a substantial amount of verbal abuse."

Even though the parents fought on a regular basis, they were unified when it came to their children. "Our mother and dad were very good at keeping us in line," says Shimon. "Between the two of them, they were very expecting of us to do our best. We were always studying hard and doing the right thing, what our parents wanted."

Bill has many of the same memories when it comes to his parents priorities for their children. "Education, education, education and, when you are done with that, have more education. My father was always embarrassed that he did not go to college; being a Depression baby, he saw that education was the key. You had to go college. From day one, whether it was second grade, fifth grade, whatever, grades were the most important thing. When we came home with A's, you could see the smile on my father's face. You couldn't do anything better than bring home good grades. My mother was not unlike that. She was more subtle, but there was no question that she expected it as well."

In a biographical essay Dennis wrote for a collegiate English class, he put into words much of what his siblings noted about the family's parent-child relationship:

There is a strong gap between my parents and the children. We can go to them for most any of our problems and we do. But my parents hold a great deal of respect and authority. They are quick to criticize, especially my father, and seldom offer rewards. This situation has been changing since I entered college three years ago; however some of the stigma of the previous relationship remains. I have had few tender moments with my parents and I remember them all.

Achievement has been the hallmark of my family. You must do your best at all times. And if your best was not good enough then you were just mediocre. Oh, how often my father used that word....

Dennis's essay also offered insights on how his parents' drive for achievement impacted their lives professionally and personally:

My mother and father are owners of a decorating business that mother is in charge of. My father is a television distributor salesman. My father is intensely concerned with the welfare of the store and will offer his advice, which is usually good, at any moment. My father is imaginative and creative but a poor manager. He treats employees with little respect. He acts as if money were the only incentive for work. My mother on the other hand creates a very favorable working atmosphere. She lends dignity and warmth to the store, and all the time she seems to be enjoying herself while she is going through a very demanding pace.... In the end my father believes that the end justifies the means (but would never consciously cheat the public). My mother concentrates on the means and justifies her ends on how she gets there—it's all in the technique.

All the Hurwitz children agree that their parents, materialistic and goal-oriented in their respective ways, were ecstatic that Steve would be an attorney and Dennis would be a doctor. It was taken for granted that Bill and Marilyn would follow their lead by making prestigious, economically viable career choices.

Shimon has a term for that kind of upbringing; he calls it the "Classic Jewish Syndrome," which he defines as "achievement, work, and enjoying life the way everybody enjoys life, from the American position, anyway."

Steve embraced the American position, until he became Shimon. The name change happened in 1973. Steve had earned his undergraduate degree at Johns Hopkins University and, adhering to the results of the aptitude test just like his brother, earned his law degree at George Washington University in 1968. Before beginning his law career, he would spend five years in the army, stationed much of the time in Korea, where he handled legal matters. Marilyn remembers that when he was in the service he became more religious, "I think maybe as a way to help with the homesickness." After his discharge, he decided to go to Israel for a month to study Hebrew prior to establishing his law practice in America.

Instead, Steve became Shimon.

He didn't just change the direction of his life, says Marilyn, he looked at his former life and the lives of his family as the wrong way to live. It was not just, "I'm going to live this way," it was, "The way you are living is wrong." He would not practice law again. Rather, he would remain in Israel and become a rabbi at a yeshiva, an institution for Torah study within Orthodox Judaism. He would spend his days as an observant Jew who would "recruit" others to become observant. "My parents were very disappointed that he did that," says Marilyn. "As a parent, I would be, too. They invested a lot of money in his education, and he goes and tosses it all. For a while, he was postulating. None of us could understand that. That created even a bigger gulf between us."

His postulating led to him writing a book that was published in 1978, *Being Jewish* (Jerusalem: Feldheim Publishers).

The book offers more than a peek at the gulf between Shimon and Steve. Chapter One begins with Shimon writing: *The core of western culture can be expressed in one idea—the individual. He is the king.* He goes on to make the point that such an existence leads a person to believe *that man is the central purpose of the world's existence and that everything should be directed to taking care of him and his needs.* Nothing could be further from the truth, according to Shimon. *That man is the center of all things is an absurdity beyond all question.... The center for the Jew is Hashem (God), the Creator and Father of all.... The Torah is the Foundation, Blueprint, and Guidebook of the Jew's existence.... The Jew gets his place in eternity according to the merit of the deeds which he has done.... Life, then, is a preparation, a practice chamber, for entrance into a life of far greater significance and lastingness.... Judaism is not a religion. It is a way of life. Not just for special occasions—bar mitzvahs, weddings, funerals—but for every second of the Jew's life.*

To Shimon, a Jew's life should consist of strict dietary laws, daily prayer, observance of Jewish festivals, and the ongoing study and adherence of Torah, which is the body of scripture known to non-Jews as the

Old Testament. It deals with everything from agricultural laws to marriage and divorce to tort laws and financial matters. He believes such a life is impossible for his family and friends unless they undergo the same kind of philosophical change he embraced. *Authentic Jewish culture and western culture are 180 degrees apart,* he states in his book's preface.

Like his brother's book written decades later, Shimon's book wasn't a best seller. It did have at least one reader, though: Dennis. He received a copy from his brother who handwrote on page one a note to Dennis and Linda:

To Den and Linda,

May this effort to explain the true meaning of being Jewish show you how much I was willing to labor in order to convince you. So I ask of you—who are so important to me—to read this book carefully and know that every word comes to help bring closer and speak to those inner yearnings which you yourselves already feel.

With love and affection,

Shimon

Proof that Dennis read the book is evident throughout the margins. He penned the following words:

False

Why?

I don't feel that way

Not so

You don't need Torah for this

Not necessarily so

Conspicuously missing are words like: yes, agreed, true, crucial, enlightening.

Missing, too, is the big brother he thought would always be there. He makes this realization with a sense of loss, of dejection, of the finality of his brother's fate. But there's more. Shimon makes him question his successes, his failures, his moments of happiness, his moments of despair. After all, what if Shimon's way of life is what God truly expects? "Whether I like it or not, I have within my family a moral and orthodox perspective that I'm confronted with in everything I do. It is right there between my eyes from the brother I shared a room with growing up, and I was closest to in my family, who happens to be a revered, well-thought-of, special rabbi in Jerusalem whose job is to save souls, so to speak, of wayward souls like me."

Dennis speaks about his brother with some pride but great hurt. For him and the rest of his family the hurt was so great that when Shimon announced he was getting married, his parents, his brothers, and his sister told him they were not going to attend.

The announcement of the pending arranged marriage came around two years after Shimon had taken his journey to Israel. On January 22, 1975, he would marry in Jerusalem a woman he met through the yeshiva rabbis. His fiancée was born in Israel, had studied in the states a couple of years. Her parents, like her future in-laws, were divorced, and she, like Shimon, chose in her late twenties to become an observant Jew.

Dennis did have second thoughts about declining to attend, especially because Linda thought it was the family's responsibility to be present, but scheduling was problematic. By this time, he had completed medical school at the University of Maryland and a two-year residency in general surgery at Yale University. Now, he, Linda, and their baby daughter, Karen, were living in Vermont as Dennis was in the final year of a three-year residency in general surgery at Dartmouth Affiliated Hospitals. "They don't give you a lot of time off," he says.

It wasn't an ideal time for his parents, either. They were in the middle of getting divorced after 31 years of marriage, but both were united in their anger that Shimon wasn't coming home and wasn't going to be an attorney.

His mom told him that she didn't approve of the marriage, but she would go to the wedding if it took place in Baltimore. Shimon didn't acquiesce. Neither did his mom or his dad. The marriage would take place with no Hurwitzes, except for the groom.

On Christmas Day, though, things changed. Dennis was skiing in New Hampshire when he fell, separating his shoulder. The doctors told him he didn't need surgery, but he couldn't work for six weeks. Suddenly, he could make the January 22 wedding.

"I said to Linda, 'We should do it; we should go to Jerusalem for Shimon's marriage.'" Linda didn't need to be convinced. She always believed they should go, even though it caused her a scheduling conflict. She taught English, half days, at the local middle school. And, as for Karen, only two years old, she would need to stay behind with a babysitter.

Linda would make the necessary arrangements. Two weeks before the wedding, Dennis gets a phone call. It's his father. "Your mother and I are going to the wedding," he tells Dennis. "I had a dream that my son got married, and I wasn't there. I realized I shouldn't do that. And I convinced your mother to go with us."

Travel arrangements were made so they could take the 12-hour flight together. To try and maintain some decorum, Linda sat between her battling in-laws. They seemed to argue about everything, except Shimon. When he was the subject, they had a plan. They were going to deprogram him and bring him back to the United States. Once they removed him from the holy aura that permeates Jerusalem, they truly believed he would come to his senses and begin his law career.

When their flight arrived in Jerusalem, they were greeted by someone they barely recognized. He wore a long coat, had long braided sideburns called *peyote* (the Torah forbids male Jews from removing hair from their sideburns), and he spoke English with almost an Eastern European accent. It was Shimon. And he, too, had great worries.

"He was an emotional wreck," says Dennis, "because he had to get us to the hotel by sundown." The Sabbath would start then, which meant an observant Jew could do no work whatsoever, and that included riding in a cab. The cab driver put Shimon's fears to rest. The trip to the hotel ended before sundown. Once they arrived, though, there was a new problem. Shimon's parents, whose civility toward each other was a distant memory, were sharing a room. It did have two beds, but that was little consolation to Mrs. Hurwitz. "My mother tacked a sheet across the room," says Dennis. Then, in her half of the room, she cried. He and Linda could hear sobs through the wall separating their rooms. "And my mother-in-law never cried," says Linda. Dennis agrees: "The only other time I heard her cry was, briefly, when she found out her mother died. That's it."

Shimon had arranged a Sabbath dinner for himself and his family at one of the yeshiva member's homes. The host seemed to disappear after everyone ate, and Shimon's parents seized the opportunity to bring Steve back to life. Dennis remembers well his parents' argument: "How can you throw away your life like this? You're not making any money, and you have all of this training, and we paid for all of this education. You're still studying, and you're 32 years old. What are you going to do with your life? This is not right for you. You can still be orthodox, but you can be a lawyer and make a living in Baltimore. You don't have to be in Jerusalem to be orthodox."

"They went after him as hard as I could imagine," says Dennis. "My parents were very dominant people. It was as if I believed they had god-like powers. Even though financially they were no wizards, I felt there was nothing they couldn't control." And, in his eyes, his parents made a very compelling argument for Shimon to return to Baltimore. "As far as I'm concerned, if this was a debate, they won. They were very effective, both of them. They said what they wanted to say. They said it strongly. They said it with confidence. I knew they made sense from my perspective."

But not from Shimon's perspective; he was no longer acting as the oldest son who always wanted to please. "Shimon stood up to them, something no one in my family ever did. I realized he really, really believed in what he was doing."

It made Dennis wonder for just a moment, "Who is right here? I wasn't pleased with my parents' wholehearted secular approach to life, but I couldn't understand Shimon's controlling world that asked for so much sacrifice. There had to be something in between."

After the great debate ended, Shimon (not Steve), Dennis, and their father stayed at the yeshiva home while Linda escorted the defeated, sobbing mother-in-law back to the hotel, trying to console the woman who never cried along the way.

"This isn't my son, this is a different person," Mrs. Hurwitz kept saying. "I just lost him forever." Linda knew that, in a way, it was true: "Shimon found a lifestyle that was going to give him an answer on how to live."

As it turns out, Dennis and Linda, more than any other couple, would need to find an answer on how to live.

Chapter Four

*D*ennis seemed to have his life figured out by 1975, at the relatively young age of 28. Unlike Shimon, he had followed the results of his career aptitude test, had married the woman he loved, and was the proud father of a baby daughter, Karen. But, the path wasn't without some eye-opening deviations.

After accepting a residency in general surgery from Yale University upon his graduation from medical school in 1970, Dennis thought his career was on track. He and Linda would settle in New Haven, Connecticut, for the foreseeable future, at least until completing his seven years of training to be a cardiac surgeon.

The United States of America, at war with Vietnam, had other ideas. Linda learned of the country's plans for her husband after a day of teaching English at the local middle school. When she returned to their New Haven apartment, she saw the official-looking sealed letter. Immediately, she opened it, even though it was addressed to Dennis. The news was unexpected. Dennis had hoped to receive a full medical-training deferment from the military. He didn't. The government chose to give him a two-year deferment.

Once his deferment would expire, in 1972, there would be no more deferments for him to declare. Most likely he would be sent to Vietnam. The two-year deferment wouldn't give him enough time in his medical training to enable him to serve in the military as a surgeon. Consequently, he probably would become a general field officer, which would put him in the line of fire in the rice patties.

Linda didn't bother passing along the unsettling news to Dennis, who was working at the hospital. Instead, clutching the letter, she drove to the nearby armory, home to the region's National Guard headquarters. She had an idea. Linda knew for months that the draft was a possibility, which is why she had been trying, unsuccessfully, to get her husband accepted in the National Guard, an alternative way to satisfy the country's military commitment. Many others had the same idea, including two men who would one day become president: Bill Clinton and George W. Bush. Dennis, though, was continually rebuffed. There was no room for him. Linda hoped and prayed on her drive to the armory that she could make the National Guard find room.

Once there, she was directed to a uniformed man behind a desk. She didn't approach him with a prepared eloquent speech. She simply spoke from the heart: "You have to take my husband, let him join the National Guard," she pleaded to him. "He just received this draft notice. Please, he can't go to Vietnam."

Maybe the uniformed man was in awe of her beauty. Maybe he could hear the newlywed panic in her voice. Maybe he didn't want to see another young man die in a war that had divided the country. Whatever it was, he said, "I'll give you the guard's enlistment papers. Take it to your husband to sign, and I'll take him in."

Linda, not sure how long the officer's good will would last, opted not to have her husband sign the papers. It might take too long to track him down. "I drove around the corner, and I signed his name to all the papers." She returned the "signed" papers to the armory, and her husband was now a member of the National Guard. "Ever since, I have to sign his name, because our handwriting is merged."

After Dennis's shift at the hospital ended, he learned from his wife how much she loved him. She had enlisted him in the National Guard. "I was on call every other night and every other weekend and, on top of that, I had one weekend a month for guard duty, and a week to 10 days every summer. Half of my vacation went to boot camp." Serving in the National Guard was not his life's ambition, but he didn't disregard his responsibility; in his 10 years of service, he rose from second lieutenant to captain.

His National Guard enlistment wasn't the only unexpected turn of events for Dennis while living in New Haven. "I actually went there with the idea of being a cardiac surgeon." He chose that specialty for a noble reason. "I looked at cardiac surgery because the technical and mental capabilities of cardiac surgeons save people's lives as opposed to neurology, which was my first interest. As intellectually stimulating as neurology is, the field is very cerebral. You can't do much more for those patients, frankly, other than to make a diagnosis and give them steroids or aspirin. I did find tumor surgery fascinating technically, but so often patients died, and that wasn't what I wanted to do with people. I didn't want to be helplessly there, cutting away at them, trying to stay ahead of a tumor that too often won out. I thought cardiac surgery would be full of dramatic, lifesaving, heroic efforts. I liked that much more."

Yale was glad he did. "At Yale, you are supposed to be tracked. After my first few months there, they asked me to stay on for seven years to finish general surgery and cardiac surgery."

He turned them down. His first rotation during his internship revealed to him that cardiac surgery wasn't as dramatic as he thought. "I discovered that cardiologists during the time of surgery were making a lot of the critical decisions—which way to go, which pump to use, or which valve to pick. To me, they seemed more like technicians, not even technicians, like plumbers. You were constantly putting tubes in, valves in; it was plumbing, that's all it was."

During his second rotation, plastic surgery began to intrigue him—it was a field that he found did more than just make repairs. He learned from Yale's chief of plastic surgery, Dr. Thomas Krizek, that plastic surgery demanded creativity, vision, decisiveness, unlimited use of imagination—it dared a surgeon to dream, and Dennis was a dreamer.

"I had no trouble quickly accepting the premise that plastic surgery was of great value to life." He had always marveled at how his mother, in her interior design business, created beauty out of a home decorating problem, which, to Dennis, paralleled the mission of a plastic surgeon.

"I like to put together things of beauty, and I believe the pursuit serves a great purpose, equivalent to that of trying to cure cancer or making a bad heart work better. It's not a life or death business, but you need plastic surgery after accidents or trauma or birth defects for people's well-being."

Other Yale residents were intrigued by the specialty, too, thanks in large part to Dr. Krizek. "He was so stimulating and made everything so interesting," says Dennis. "I was almost spellbound by him and what he portrayed plastic surgery to be—thinking of solutions in a three-dimensional, artistic way, which I was programmed to do through my mother, and figuring out what was the best way for the correction of deformity using the available technical knowledge. He was like a pied piper. A lot of interns who went through Yale underwent a transformation like I did."

In fact, of the dozen or so residents in 1972, nearly half sought the plastic surgery track, which meant completing general surgery and then specializing in plastic surgery. "Yale didn't want to funnel that many through," he says. Owing to his late interest in the specialty, Dennis wasn't selected. Dr. Krizek, upon learning of the university's decision, offered the resident a one-year research fellowship, which helped assuage in Dennis any feelings of inadequacy. Also, he could reapply the following year, but there would be no guarantees. "That was the first time I really didn't get what I wanted, the first time. I remember it as being devastating. I never had to deal with that before."

He didn't wallow in his misfortune. He chose to move forward by asking one of the senior surgeons what he should do—stay at Yale, do the research, and hope to resume his general surgery residency the following year, or, instead, look elsewhere. The surgeon told him that, without a guarantee from Yale, he should pursue other options. It proved to be good advice. There were still a few fall 1972 general surgery openings available from prestigious medical centers around the country. "Very good opportunities," remembers Dennis.

So, in the late winter, early spring of 1972 he was on the interview trail. One of the first stops was the University of Pittsburgh, which had been recommended to him by another of his Yale colleagues. He told Dennis that Pitt had a very strong plastic surgery program and would provide him with excellent training." Dennis heeded the advice and met with the university's department chair, Dr. William L. White, who must have been impressed. He informally offered Dennis a senior residency in plastic surgery, where he could train and be a member of that renowned department. There was one caveat, though. He first had to complete his general surgery residency, and the university didn't have space for another general surgeon resident.

Shut out of Yale and Pitt, Dennis remained undaunted and continued on the interview trail. He soon found an Ivy League replacement for his general surgery residency. "Dartmouth didn't, at the time, have a training program in plastic surgery, but it had very good, high quality plastic surgery." Dennis believed he would receive significant plastic surgery operating experience there. Just as he accepted Pitt's informal offer, he didn't hesitate in saying yes to Dartmouth and remembers feeling "forever grateful" that he was given the opportunity to continue his medical training on a path that seemed the most practical, given his chosen specialty.

Linda was not so grateful. She was sad to leave the vibrant New Haven town where she had made many good friends and was a mere five-hour train ride from her parents. In addition, life was getting complicated. On May 4, 1972, she became a mom, giving birth to a daughter, whom Dennis and Linda would name Karen Rachel, but not before some unusual discussion.

In Jewish tradition, babies are named in memory of a deceased loved one. Linda and Dennis originally wanted their daughter's first name to be Stephanie, an anglicized version of the Polish name Stefcha, for Linda's Aunt Stefcha, who died in the Holocaust. "My mother wouldn't let me," says Linda, "because she said her sister died too young and too tragically." The objection made sense; Jewish tradition also enjoins parents to name their babies after people who lived a long, happy, healthy life. That was not the case with Stefcha, so Linda and Dennis acquiesced. They

Chapter Four

chose the name Karen, in part, after the character Linda admired in one of her favorite books, the 1958 classic, *Exodus*, by Leon Uris. That book is described by a *New York Times* review as the *passionate summary of the inhuman treatment of the Jewish people in Europe, of the exodus in the nineteenth and twentieth centuries to Palestine, and of the triumphant founding of the new Israel.* The book's character, Karen, was a "beautiful, gentle, sweet, young woman," says Linda, not recalling at the time that by the end of the story, Karen Hansen Clement, who survived the Holocaust and immigrated to Israel, was stabbed to death by terrorists. It was certainly an ominous namesake.

Choosing a middle name was much more uneventful. Dennis's mother asked that they remember her mother. The parents gladly agreed to do so, and the first grandchild for all four grandparents on either side became Karen Rachel Hurwitz.

Karen, born two weeks before Linda's due date, almost preempted her mother's Master of Arts degree from Southern Connecticut State College. "I just turned in my thesis right before she was born," says Linda. "I wrote it on Richard Wright, the black writer." She's not exactly sure why. She was impressed with Wright's work, but some of her favorite writers at the time were Ernest Hemingway, Philip Roth, and Leon Uris. Perhaps the attraction to Mr. Wright was her empathy for the suffering of African Americans, somewhat similar to the injustices toward her Jewish ancestors decimated by the Holocaust? Perhaps it was something else entirely? For whatever reason, she simply found herself drawn to Wright. "My thesis was *Violence as a Source of Self-Identity in the Black Male Character.*"

New degree. New baby. And now there would be a new home. When the time came for her six-week, post-delivery checkup, it was just two weeks before their July 1 moving date to Vermont. At the doctor's appointment, they discussed birth control. "He asked, 'What do you want to do now?' He mentioned several options. The IUD sounded like a great idea. You put it in for a year, have it taken out, and have another kid. That is what I did."

A few days later, she was doubled over in pain.

"By the time I went to the emergency room, I thought it was a gall-bladder attack or something. I never really saw my gynecologist, because we were moving. Everybody kept saying you're probably having some post-delivery infection. Obviously, I had an infection. Nobody was connecting it to the IUD, except for my mother, who told me not to have it in the first place."

She still had symptoms after the move and quickly found a gynecologist in Vermont. After her new doctor examined her, he told her he believed the IUD indeed was causing the problem, and he recommended its removal. Linda agreed. One problem. They couldn't find it.

"I had an infection; it caused a pelvic inflammatory disease. They didn't know if the IUD had embedded and was still in there causing the infection or not. We didn't have MRIs at that time. The hope was that I had expelled it, and, once the inflamed tissue healed, he believed I probably could get pregnant again." Such news was sobering for Dennis and Linda, who hoped Karen would have a few siblings, but they tried to remain optimistic that permanent damage hadn't been done to Linda's reproductive organs.

Health problems weren't Linda's only concerns. She was worried about life in Vermont. Neither of them had ever stepped foot in that part of the country, and it wasn't what Linda had in mind when she went for a ride in Dennis's GTO convertible. Dennis tried to romanticize the move by talking about renting a little log cabin in the woods, but his wife didn't find the imagery very appealing. "I am a Baltimore city Jewish girl. I don't belong in a log cabin in the woods. I never even saw beans growing. I grew up in row houses in Baltimore."

She was used to walking out her front door and having restaurants, museums, theaters, and her family nearby. Front doors in Vermont open to snow, mountains, trees, and wilderness. Still, it might have been romantic if she and Dennis could have gone for long walks together, or squeezed into a swaying hammock, or discovered friends throughout the country-

Chapter Four

side. But the study of medicine and National Guard duty didn't leave Dennis much room for a life outside of his daily routine.

"I tried to have empathy for what he was going through, but it was really hard," says Linda. "He was just away all the time."

At least she wasn't stuck in a log cabin. When they first arrived, they stumbled upon a small development of about 10 townhouses; one was for rent. They didn't need to contemplate the decision. The Hurwitzes had their New England home, and it provided them with some instant friends. Three other couples with young children were in the development.

"They came with the same mentality that 'I am not ready to live in a log cabin where there are bears knocking on my door,'" says Linda. "We young mothers became a great support group. We taught one another to cook in a wok, to bake bread from scratch, to play the card game bridge. We babysat for each other, had tea or coffee together many mornings, and had group exploration trips. Thank goodness we lived in that development; it was a very enriching time in many ways."

In more ways, though, it was far from newlywed paradise, especially with Dennis working so hard in his general surgery residency. "The hours are really grueling," says Dennis.

"Actually," says Linda, "he worked harder in New Haven for his Yale residency, but I was more occupied there. I was teaching, getting my master's in English. At Dartmouth, I was home with the baby, and he was never there. I just felt really frustrated, and I had already gone through the two years of his internship at Yale."

In order to have some intellectual stimulation, she decided to begin a book club. She placed notices in mailboxes, inviting women who liked to read to come to her home for a literary gathering. About a dozen women showed up on the day and time, and most became monthly members, says Linda. The first book she chose for discussion was Sylvia Plath's *The Bell Jar* (New York: Harper and Row). On the cover's inside flap, the book is described as *a comic but painful statement of what happens to a woman's*

aspirations in a society that refuses to take them seriously. "That shows you my state of mind," says Linda.

Nevertheless, Linda did her best to be a good mother and wife, which included, one night, inviting over for dinner the chief attending physician from Dennis's hospital. Once her husband's boss and his wife arrived, Linda did her best to entertain them, while anxiously awaiting Dennis to come home from work. She didn't want to serve the main course without him there. So, she waited and waited some more. Finally, dinner was served—without Dennis.

"He never showed up," says Linda, "until the end of the evening."

Another night, he came home very late on what had been a cold, dreary day. Linda was in bed, exhausted from a taxing time with baby Karen. She greeted her husband with a punch in the stomach, and it wasn't playful. "I was so exasperated. Then he told me about his patient, someone had shot himself, and I felt horrible."

The patient died despite Dennis's extended efforts. These kinds of day-to-day, real-life dramas took their toll on him. When his workday ended, he sought refuge at home. One question he never wanted to hear from Linda was, "How was your day, dear?" He just wanted to rest and re-invigorate himself with the simplicity of home before beginning the next day's hospital routine. "I was taking out colons, manning the emergency room, putting patients on heart bypass, trying to put valves in."

"Part of me really did understand the pressure and responsibility he had," says Linda, "but emotionally I was just frustrated. We were leading parallel lives. With me not working and being home with Karen, I needed even more stimulation and sharing and discussion. But he would come home so tired and not even want to talk about what he was doing. He certainly didn't feel like hearing about what I was reading or thinking. He always encouraged me to do my own activities, as long as they didn't interfere with him. I started to feel isolated. I was doing everything myself. People don't know that side of being married to a doctor in training. It is really hard."

Chapter Four

Her frustration intensified during the December 1973 holidays. Linda missed her family. She decided she and Karen would go home. Home was Baltimore. "I was really thinking about not coming back," she says.

In part, the burgeoning women's movement made her view life differently. "There was an evolution I was going through. I was reading all of this angry literature. It was a time of revolution. I looked at Dennis's sister, who is four years younger than I am, she was in college, and it was totally different for her. Suddenly, there were no curfews; boys and girls were in the dorm together, and she was wearing jeans. I didn't even own a pair of jeans. The expected pattern of grown-up life had been so much more regimented and prescribed. Then, all of a sudden, I'm reading about kids doing a lot of different experimental and independent activities. I'm left feeling like I sort of missed it. I have a baby, and I'm all of 25 years old."

Dennis had no idea that his wife's angst was so profound. "I thought she was going to visit her parents for a few weeks," says Dennis. "No big deal." He survived without his family, but not without a crisis. The dishwasher broke. When all of the dishes were dirty, he had a solution; he bought paper plates.

Meanwhile, Linda talked to her father about her marriage. Her father had an unimaginable experience in coping with reality. Born a European Jew, living through World War I and the Russian Revolution, he reached adulthood about the same time Adolph Hitler had seized power. He did survive the Holocaust. His wife and two young sons did not. Nor did the rest of his family. He eventually remarried; his bride was another Holocaust survivor who lost all her immediate family and many aunts, uncles, and cousins. The adult orphans moved to the United States where Linda and her two brothers were born. The marital problems Linda faced must have seemed microscopic in comparison to what he and his wife had to endure. His reaction to Linda's distress was brief but telling.

"Does he beat you?" he asked.

"No."

The Chase for Beauty

"Does he cheat on you?"

"No."

"Then, you have to go back and work it out."

So, she returned to the dirty dishes. She also returned with a new outlook. "I knew I wasn't happy, but I realized I could not rely on him to make me happy."

Linda made changes in her life. Wore jeans. Enrolled in classes. Continued hosting her book club. Began teaching English again, half days at the middle school. That meant leaving Karen with a babysitter and not feeling guilty. "I felt much better," she says. "I realized I was the kind of person who really needs to work. I tried my two years at home without working. It wasn't for me."

Dennis noticed the change in his wife from an aesthetic standpoint. "She dressed simply with very little makeup. It was part of that Betty Friedan, Gertrude Stein feminist culture. Women weren't supposed to use their beauty as an exceptionally attractive force." Dennis didn't mind. "She still looked beautiful."

Their marriage was once again on a tenure track. So was Dennis's medical career. He completed his general surgery residency, which meant he could officially accept the plastic surgery residency offer from the University of Pittsburgh. As the Hurwitzes packed their bags for the move, life was good. All that was missing was more children, but Dennis and Linda held out hope that Karen, nearly three years old, would have a brother or sister very soon. With their love for each other, their faith in the future, and their belief in a life that Shimon shunned but Dennis's parents admired, the Hurwitzes arrived in Pittsburgh in the late spring of 1975, thinking they were ready for whatever would happen next.

Chapter Five

Pittsburgh seemed like a good match for the Hurwitzes. In some ways, the city is similar to Baltimore. Geographically, it is more East Coast than Midwest, though when the East Coast comes to mind, the cities New York; Boston; Philadelphia; Washington, DC; and Baltimore are the ones that stand out. Pittsburgh, which evolved at the convergence of the Ohio, Monongahela, and Allegheny rivers, does not. "Until I interviewed there, I didn't even know where it was," says Dennis.

Although it may not have a thriving urban reputation, it looks like very much like an East Coast city—central downtown, classic architecture, ethnic neighborhoods. It feels like an East Coast city, too—cultural, proud, intense. But, by being located in between the Atlantic Coast and St. Louis's Gateway to the Midwest, it has an image problem that probably gives it a bit of an identity crisis. The lack of notoriety may be what makes it more determined than most cities to define itself. Perhaps that is why throughout the first half of the 20th century it dominated the steel industry that enabled industrialized America to be built; and why, at the outset of the century, it gave birth to labor unions that helped protect the rights of those who would build America; and why, at the start of the second half of the century, it was where the polio vaccine originated, which would protect the country from a devastating illness that knew no social boundaries. It's a city that took great pride in nurturing the likes of Andrew Carnegie, George Westinghouse, and Jonas Salk.

This city, with an East Coast diversity, a Midwestern work ethic, and European neighborhood friendliness, became home to the Hurwitzes. They wasted little time in settling. The University of Pittsburgh and its medical complex are just a few miles east of the downtown, in the university-dominated Oakland section. The Hurwitzes, well beyond their collegiate days, opted to consider apartments in one of two neighborhoods adjoining Oakland—Shadyside and Squirrel Hill. Shadyside is Pittsburgh's mini-answer to Washington, DC's, Georgetown. At its center is Walnut Street, a small thoroughfare of eclectic shops, restaurants, and bars. This hub is surrounded by several blocks of predominantly young doctors, lawyers, professionals, and artists living in an impressive array of classic brownstones and other vintage homes, some beautifully rehabbed, others for more bohemian lifestyles. From a brick and mortar standpoint, Shadyside's neighbor, Squirrel Hill, looks roughly the same. It's the cars that reveal a big difference. In Squirrel Hill, parked on the streets and in the garages were station wagons, not two-seat convertibles.

There is another difference, too: temples and synagogues. Squirrel Hill has a collection of them: Reform, Conservative, Orthodox. While much of the city's Jewish population lives throughout the East End, which includes Oakland, Shadyside, and Squirrel Hill, clearly the Jewish anchor is Squirrel Hill, Pittsburgh's combination of Brooklyn and Long Island.

After arriving in Pittsburgh, the Hurwitz's Chevrolet Malibu ended up getting parked at a two-bedroom townhouse in Shadyside. "I loved it," says Linda. "Here I was, back in the city; I could walk to Walnut Street."

From there, Dennis's commute to the hospital in Oakland took only a few minutes, as was Linda's commute to Chatham College and Rodef Shalom temple, where she taught courses in women's literature. Not to be outdone, Karen's commute to the Jewish Community Center preschool in Squirrel Hill could be measured in minutes, too.

They were strangers in their latest hometown, but not for long. Dennis and Linda turned to their religion. With so many Jewish congregations to choose from, they began trying them out one by one. On Friday nights, they started attending Sabbath services at different congregations. On the Friday when they seated themselves in the sanctuary at Tree of Life synagogue, a native Pittsburgher, Harvey Wolsh and his wife, Carole, noticed the newcomers. After the service, the members socialized while enjoying

The Chase for Beauty

coffee and pastries. The Wolshes, a few years older than the Hurwitzes, introduced themselves. Linda made sure the introduction led to a conversation. The couples talked about Baltimore. They talked about Pittsburgh. They talked about Karen and the two Wolsh children. They talked about their professions.

Dennis didn't merely mention that he was a plastic surgeon; he talked about how he wanted to save lives. He would do all he could to help people with any kind of disfigurement from being ostracized, from being persecuted, from being emotionally destroyed. Mr. Wolsh, an accountant, found the newcomer's passion very engaging. "I like to think I'm a good judge of character, and I could see right away that Dennis was a hardworking, driven person. He was consumed with plastic surgery, determined to do something special."

Nobody wanted the evening to end. "They were starting to clean up," remembers Mr. Wolsh, "so Linda invited us over to their apartment that night. We just hit it off."

The Hurwitzes were no longer strangers in a new city. Linda would make sure that their new friends would be the first of many. She began forming friendships with the mothers in her literature classes and the parents of Karen's preschool classmates. "They weren't only doctors' wives, like in Vermont, which was really nice," says Linda. She and Dennis started having more and more weekend plans with their expanding circle of friends, many of whom had the same heritage, which was a refreshing change for Linda: "With the families from the JCC, most of them were Jewish. It was this comfort level, an ease, a feeling of familiarity and belonging, compared to being up in Dartmouth, where we made lovely friends but never felt quite as comfortable. Suddenly, we were friendly with all these nice Jewish couples with kids the same age. It was fun; that helps you like a place."

She seemed very content in Pittsburgh, drawn to its values, its compassion, its peacefulness. Dennis, too, had found a welcome home at the University of Pittsburgh's plastic surgery department, a department that, he learned at Yale, was well respected throughout the country.

Dr. Ross Musgrave, one of the department's legendary surgeons, was very pleased with the new plastic surgery resident. "It was plain for all of us to see that Dennis had a real gift for surgery, very capable hands," he says. "He wasn't afraid to make the bold decisions, to try new techniques." Dr. Musgrave's primary worry about Dennis centered on what would happen to him if something went wrong while performing an innovative procedure. "I worried about his vulnerability."

Dennis didn't harbor such worries. Life was moving forward much like he imagined it would. The one significant glitch was adding to his family. The hope that Linda's IUD fiasco only caused ephemeral damage to her fallopian tubes was beginning to seem exceedingly optimistic.

She had surgery at Magee-Womens Hospital in Pittsburgh to try to undo the damage from the scar tissue caused by her pelvic inflammatory condition in 1972. "We had no way of knowing if it was successful," says Linda. "We just had to wait and see." The wait wasn't passive. Linda began taking fertility drugs—first clomiphene, then pergonal, in hopes of medically stimulating the release of hormones necessary for ovulation to occur. She also maintained a body temperature chart to try and determine when she ovulated.

Initially, neither the operation, nor the drugs, nor the temperature chart led to the moment where Karen's mom and dad could tell her that she was going to have a baby sister or brother.

They tried not to let the inability to conceive again consume them. "We were living our lives," says Linda. "We had Karen, and Dennis and I are very adult oriented. As much as we wanted kids, because you're supposed to want kids, we really wanted it more for Karen, so she could have siblings. But there are also advantages to being an only child. She got to travel a lot with us. It's easy to pick up and go with one."

Professionally, Dennis hadn't encountered failure of any significance since being denied the Yale residency. On the contrary, he was completely enamored with his chosen field. He couldn't learn enough about the latest techniques, articles, and case studies. One breakthrough, occurring across the Atlantic Ocean, particularly caught his attention. A French plastic surgeon, Paul Tessier, had been busy publishing papers and making presentations about a new procedure called craniofacial surgery. His approach and findings garnered worldwide acclaim.

"Craniofacial pertains to the head and face, and craniofacial surgery involves delicate procedures to rebuild or replace facial bones and tissues," explains Dennis. Patients who could benefit from this plastic surgery specialty include people who had serious facial injuries or abnormal growths from tumors or people born with deformities such as cleft lips, ear deformities, or misshapen jaws. Craniofacial surgery can involve bone, skin, muscle, and teeth.

Dr. Tessier, whose last name is pronounced without the "R" sound, began publicizing his technique for correcting craniofacial disorders in the late '60s and early '70s. Before then, Dennis says there was no uniform, widely accepted approach to the problem. Tessier's techniques are based on the principle that the bones must be repositioned or reconstructed before the soft tissue can be repaired, a revolutionary departure from the established standard of care.

"Paul Tessier," says Dennis, "had taken the field and given a name to it. Before him, if somebody was injured and had his skull bashed in, a neurosurgeon would work together with a plastic surgeon, but until Dr. Tessier's articles, there really wasn't a term for that—the deliberate, planned effort to rebuild the face in a planned, teamwork way." The plastic surgeon reconstructs the facial deformity while the neurosurgeon is primarily concerned with the cranial deformity. Combining the expertise of the plastic surgeon and neurosurgeon created far better aesthetic results than what had been previously considered an acceptable outcome.

Dennis read some of Tessier's most significant articles while he was in his second (and final) year of residency at Pitt. The Frenchman's ideas more than caught the Pittsburgh resident's attention. "I read everything I could about it," says Dennis, finding himself mesmerized by the specialty. "I liked the idea that whatever you did was going to be new, and I felt that the face was the most fascinating part of plastic surgery. To me, the essence of what plastic surgery is about is facial appearance. It is about beauty. To help deformed kids, well, I just wanted to do it."

He gave no thought or concern to the economic implications, which he says may have been for the best. "The specialty doesn't pay that well."

Dennis continued to stay abreast of every article by Dr. Tessier and others on craniofacial surgery. His knowledge didn't go to waste. His turn to present at Grand Rounds turn was coming. At the University of Pittsburgh, and most other medical institutions, Grand Rounds is a regular meeting of the academic physicians. During the session, a staff member, or invited guest, hosts a discussion regarding the latest information or breakthrough of a medical topic or issue challenging the community. At Pitt, residents were among those asked to make such presentations.

When it came time for Dennis to present at Grand Rounds, he knew his subject: craniofacial surgery. What he didn't know was that his boss, Dr. White, was in the midst of a political battle. "The oral surgeons and the neurosurgeons wanted to team up and start doing craniofacial surgery," says Dennis. Plastic surgeons weren't in the mix. To Dr. White, the chair of the plastic surgery department, that couldn't have been welcome news, especially in light of Dr. Tessier's pioneering techniques in the field. He had protested to the chief of neurosurgery, which prompted their boss, Henry Bahnson, the professor of surgery and department chair at the medical school, to intervene. In essence, he told Dr. White that if he didn't like the arrangement, then he should suggest a craniofacial surgeon from his department who would be willing to perform the operations. It seemed like a fair solution, except that none of the university's well-established plastic surgeons had training in Dr. Tessier's methods.

Then came Dennis's Grand Rounds presentation. After it was over, Dr. White pulled him aside, put his arm around him, and asked: "What do you want to do with this craniofacial surgery?"

Dennis stumbled for a moment and then said, "I think I have to go somewhere and learn about it."

"I'll see what I can do with you working with this guy Tessier," replied Dr. White, who pronounced the "R" in Tessier's name. "It's not that he didn't know how to pronounce his name," says Dennis. "Willie White was bigger than life, and he would call Tessier whatever he wanted to."

There was one stipulation that Dr. White quickly added after making his offer to Dennis: "I expect you to come back to Pittsburgh and practice here."

Dr. White was nearing retirement after having a long, illustrious career in plastic surgery. Taking that into consideration, Dennis figured his boss had many connections in the field, and that there was a very good possibility Dr. White would secure a fellowship for him with Dr. Tessier. That meant a commitment to Pittsburgh.

Dennis and Linda had a talk that evening. The conversation didn't take long. Linda, as always, supported her husband: "Well, you want to do it; Pittsburgh's okay, we've made some good friends, it's a nice town."

From Dennis's perspective, always competitive, it didn't hurt that the city's professional sports teams were doing well. In football, the Steelers had won the Super Bowl. "They were a dynasty." And, in major league baseball, "the Pirates weren't so bad, either" having won the World Series in 1971. They came to a quick agreement that Pittsburgh would become their permanent home if Dr. White offered Dennis a chance to learn from Dr. Tessier.

He didn't. "I can't get you a job with Tessier," he told Dennis just a few days after Dennis had his talk with Linda. Before Dennis had a chance to feel disappointed, Dr. White told him about another doctor based in Mexico, Dr. Fernando Ortiz Monasterio, who agreed to mentor Dennis. Along with Dr. Tessier, Dr. Monasterio was considered a pioneer in the developing field. He was chief of staff of the Plastic and Reconstructive Surgery Unit of Mexico City's Hospital General Manuel Gea González. He was also the coordinator of the National [Mexican] Program for the detection and attention of Craniofacial Anomalies. And, at the age of 53, he had been performing craniofacial surgery for six years, since 1970. Dennis was familiar with Dr. Monasterio and impressed with his work.

Dr. White reminded Dennis of his stipulation: "You can't go there too long, three or four months; then you need to come back here. Will you come?"

Dennis didn't have much to consider. "There weren't any fellowships out there for craniofacial surgery. There were just a couple of places you could go to learn and that was it; it was just so new."

He accepted Dr. White's offer without hesitation. "Willie liked that; he was that kind of man. We didn't talk about it again. No contract. No nothing."

By late spring of 1977, Dennis was on the verge of completing his residency with still nothing guaranteed in writing from Pitt. Finally, Dennis approached Dr. White. "Dr. White, what are the arrangements here?"

"Well, you're going to train with Fernando."

"But Dr. White, Fernando doesn't pay."

"I'll loan you $3,000, and you can pay it back."

"Okay," replied Dennis, a bit befuddled. "When I come back do you want me to work in your office?" Dr. White had a private practice in addition to his academic work.

"No, Dennis."

"Why?"

"I don't want someone in my office who knows more about something in plastic surgery than I do."

They both laughed. Dennis didn't know if he really meant it or not, but he never did invite him to work in his office. Dennis did accept an academic clinical position at Pitt that paid $52,000 annually, quite a raise from his $12,000 resident's salary. Before his first paycheck, he, Linda, and Karen were off to Mexico City for a summer in Zona Rosa.

The Chase for Beauty

Chapter Six

In the summer of 1972, Linda worried about living in an area so desolate that bears might knock on her family's front door. Five years later, she was living in a city bursting at its seams with people. Population numbers vary depending on the source, but after the number exceeds 10 million, does the exact number really matter anyway? Mexico City is crowded. It's polluted. It's beautiful. It's big. It's historic. It's poor. It's wealthy. And for the summer of 1977, it's home to Linda, Dennis, and Karen.

The only way a bear could knock on their front door would be to first climb a set of stairs. The Hurwitzes lived above a restaurant in the famed Zona Rosa, which, for gringos, translates into the Pink Zone. Their summer home wasn't completely foreign to their Shadyside digs. The scale, though, must be multiplied exponentially. Everywhere were restaurants, handicraft markets, antiques stores, and night clubs. Models, beggars, tourists, artists, business executives, and an assortment of rodents were just part of the cast that shared Reforma Avenue and the other Zona Rosa thoroughfares.

At first, Linda had little difficulty adjusting to life south of the border. She enjoyed the historic sites. Karen, on the other hand, found that experiencing her third universe in five years was unnerving. "She hung to us like glue," says Dennis.

Her dad wasn't around that much to latch onto, though. He wasn't there for a summer vacation or to sightsee. Dr. Monasterio kept him, and all his trainees, very busy. "There were times some summers," recollects Dr. Monasterio, "that there were so many doctors from Europe, sometimes I would have 20 people around me in the operating room, but this is the way it went. I gave Dennis the opportunity that I gave to everybody. He would scrub with me and work all day. Long, long days working."

The sheer number of people in the operating room was a new experience for Dennis. "In the world of Central America, South America, the Iberian Peninsula, all of the Spanish-speaking world for sure—the Italians, too, he was it," says Dennis. "They were there all the time. They would stack stools on top of tables, so they could see him. It was like an amphitheater. He was in his heyday."

Dennis quickly realized why his trainer—who spoke French, English, Italian, and Spanish eloquently— was so revered and why Dr. White thought him to be a more than adequate replacement for Dr. Tessier. "Fernando had phenomenal hand-eye coordination, the best hands I've ever seen in surgery. The best. He could look at tissue in the OR, go to maybe the ear and carve something out of the ear and put it in the nose, and it would fit like it was made to go there. He had the ability, the aesthetic eye, to see what was needed and how to do it efficiently."

Dr. Monasterio felt obligated to train as many surgeons as possible, because he believed maxillofacial and oral surgeons had no business operating in craniofacial cases. "I don't call them surgeons," he says. "I call them dentists. In my institution they won't do any more surgery as long as I live. They hate me. They don't like me. I say, 'I'm the surgeon, you're just a dentist.' I won't accept them. They will call me when they have the MD degree; it doesn't make any difference. 'You have not done general surgery. You are not a surgeon. Maybe I will be very happy to have you do general surgery without the MD degree. I don't care about the MD degree. It is the fact that you have to be a surgeon.'"

Like Dr. Musgrave, Dr. White, and the other University of Pittsburgh plastic surgeons, Dr. Monasterio quickly determined that Dennis met his *you have to be a surgeon* criteria. "My first impression was that he was nice, hardworking young man, wanting to learn craniofacial surgery—see and do the techniques." His impression didn't change once he saw Dennis in the operating room. "He does very good work."

The mentor and protégé bonded, and not just in the operating room.

"We got along very well," says Dr. Monasterio. "We became friends, and I invited him to sail with me on the weekends as a guest at my country home. There is a beautiful lake, good wind every year, lots of dinghy racing, and I became very keen of that, actually."

Dr. Monasterio thrived on competition. He sailed a one-man boat, representing Mexico, in the 1964 Olympic Summer Games, held in Tokyo. He didn't win, but that didn't mean he was content losing. He is considered by many who know him, including Dennis and Linda, to be a renaissance man, and he didn't do anything with the intention of coming in second place. Not at the Olympics and not at the weekend two-man sailboat races at Valle de Bravo Lake.

Dennis, who learned to sail while at Dartmouth, knew his mentor's expectations when he accepted his invitation to "crew" for him at an upcoming weekend race.

It was an invitation that Dennis didn't take lightly. First, he felt honored that he, Linda, and Karen would be guests at Dr. Monasterio's country home, a home so beautiful that it was featured in *Architectural Digest* magazine. Secondly, he knew that Dr. Monasterio had his choice of helmsmen. The guest didn't want to let his host down. Dr. Monasterio's competitive streak didn't offend Dennis. After all, he didn't like losing, either.

For both of them to have a satisfying weekend, they would have to beat around 40 other 14-foot sailboats in the one-nautical-mile race. Their start wasn't ideal; they planned to go shore side and ended up having to sneak behind some of the fleet to get there. Dennis was in constant motion, controlling the jib and mainsail. Once they established their position, the skipper realized they had "good clean air" from the 20-knot southeasterly wind, and he told his crew of one that they needed to "hike out." Through their use of the sails, they began to distance themselves from all but a few of the other boats. As they rounded the final buoy, there were still enough boats in contention to prevent anyone from feeling safe about who would win. The skipper and helmsman with surgical hands were leaning so far out of their vessel that they could have capsized. They didn't, though. What their leaning did do was allow their sail to harness the maximum amount of wind.

"We didn't lose," says Dennis, which to both of them may have been their driving force. It's not so much that they wanted to win, it's that they hated to lose—on the lake, on the tennis courts, on the ski slopes, and in the operating room.

For Dennis, things were going as well in the operating room as they did on the lake. During a particular operation on one of Dr. Monasterio's craniofacial patients, Dennis—who was scrubbed in and assisting—noticed the patient's teeth weren't aligning properly. He consulted with the orthodontist and solved the problem. Dr. Monasterio was duly impressed at the young surgeon's initiative and results. The $3,000 loan by Dr. White to have Dennis train with Dr. Monasterio was proving to be a wise move.

Dennis wasn't the only one benefiting from the stay in Mexico. So was his extended family. They were invited to experience a culture from another part of the world. Dennis's sister, Marilyn, accepted the invitation, as did Linda's younger brother, Allen, and her mother, Irene Furst.

During each of their stays, the Hurwitzes, including 5-year-old Karen, took their guests to some nearby sightseeing spots that Linda had discovered. Mrs. Furst remembers holding tightly to her granddaughter's hand when they visited Calzada de los Muertos, which Linda told her meant the Avenue of the Dead. The avenue is the main thoroughfare of Teotihuacan, which is on the outskirts of Mexico City. Historians say the haunting name derived from the Aztec tribe, who believed the modest temples, bordering both sides of the avenue, were actually tombs of kings or priests. Linda noted to her mom that the avenue's Pyramid of the Sun is the third-largest pyramid in the world; only two in Egypt are larger. She also talked about the sacred meaning of the steps leading to nowhere, which are throughout the ancient grounds.

The Hurwitz group was hardly alone in viewing the artifacts from an ancient civilization. Tourists were everywhere in what has become one of Mexico City's most popular sightseeing destinations. Yet, as they walked though the mystical grounds, Mrs. Furst wasn't a tourist; she was a grandmother:

"Karen was holding on to me, I remember." The talk of tombs, of falling saints, of the dead, had scared her granddaughter.

"Am I going to die?" Karen asked.

"No, Karen; you're not going to die," her grandmother reassured her. "Don't even think about it."

Karen didn't seem to find solace in her grandmother's words. "She was so afraid that she was going to die. She was obsessed with the thought of dying," says Mrs. Furst. "I promised her that she would not die young."

Her grandmother's calming words finally helped, but not completely. It was as if she had some kind of premonition. "Karen was very insecure in Mexico City," says Mrs. Furst. "I think she was overwhelmed with a busy, very-very-busy city. She had lived in Vermont, don't forget."

Linda did her best to make sure that her daughter had some good memories of Mexico, too. About a month into the summer, the sightseeing started to lose its luster, so Linda took Karen to Mexico City's Jewish Community Center. Unfortunately, she learned that the center's guests needed to be sponsored by existing members, much like a country club in the United States. Linda knew no one, but, drawing on the same resolve that got her through Dennis's draft notice, she pleaded with the guard in charge:

"Just let me in for a day, and I'll find someone to sponsor me."

Perhaps it was her beauty paying dividends again, her sweet but persuasive brown eyes, because the guard relented. Once inside, Karen started playing at the swimming pool with another young girl about the same age. It turned out both Karen's friend and her mother spoke English. They were from Boston, and, by day's end, they became the Hurwitz's sponsor and friends. Karen had a playmate for the rest of the summer, and that spawned new poolside friendships, but it also spawned a problem. With her short haircut, some of the children thought she was a boy. "In Mexico, the way to tell little boys from little girls is earrings," says Dennis. Karen's ears weren't pierced.

"They call me Niño, Dad, and I'm a Niña. I need earrings."

For Karen, it was one of those times when it was a bonus to have a dad who was a plastic surgeon. In a matter of moments, Karen could wear earrings.

Linda happened to make other acquaintances outside the JCC, including an American bachelor who happened to be living in the apartment above the Hurwitzes. Dennis remembers him well. "He wanted to seduce my wife," he says. "He told her so." Such a remark, while intended to be humorous, could still spark jealousy in most husbands. Not in Dennis, though. He didn't find the stranger's attraction to his wife's beauty insulting or threatening. He construed it as a compliment:

"There's a song that says, 'If you want to be happy for the rest of your life, never make a pretty woman your wife.' I took the other turn. I could only be happy marrying a beautiful woman; but you have to take the shit. And the shit is I'm not the only one who appreciates the beauty. I know it, but I rely on her character to get rid of these suitors and my ability to keep her interested in me. I never lost faith in that."

Linda did not find her admirer unattractive. His romantic interest, feigned or real, came at an interesting time in the Hurwitz marriage. Linda, in her correspondence with some of her Pittsburgh friends, learned that there were some marital problems brewing for a few couples who frequently socialized with the Hurwitzes. "Lots of stuff was going on at home," says Linda, "It was the time of *Bob & Carol & Ted & Alice*. All of us had married young, and all of us were torn between staying committed and fooling around. I remember writing to one of my friends about the composite of all the roles we women play. *I'm a daughter, I'm a mother, I'm a wife, I'm a friend, and the sum of the whole is greater than the parts.*" For Linda, one of the parts wasn't an adulterer.

"Think about it," says Dennis. "She's in Mexico away from all her links, and she is still faithful. If ever there was a time to be unfaithful, she could have done it. It's almost too good to be true that she was faithful. We're a love story." And, with a bit of self-criticism, he adds, "I just shrug it off like a jerk."

As the Hurwitz's departure from Mexico neared, they had to stretch what was left of the $3,000 loan from Dr. White by eating more chicken quesadillas than they care to remember. That culinary plight, and the awkwardness and enrapture of living in a different culture, all seemed insignificant in comparison to what Dennis says he learned about being a surgeon:

"Aside from learning the craft of craniofacial surgery, learning aesthetic surgery, rhinoplasty in particular, the most indelible impression I had was of the lifestyle of the plastic surgeons there, including my host. It was incredible hard work, like nothing I had ever seen in this country. Those who are the movers and pushers—the brightest like Fernando— they typically do what is common in most every country outside of the United States."

With a sense of admiration and humility, Dennis recounts his international colleagues' typical workday. It began in the hospital around sunrise. The surgeons would be operating, checking on patients, or working in the clinic. By mid-afternoon, it was time for a siesta. "Except, they didn't siesta," Dennis emphatically clarifies. Rather than resting, the surgeons traveled to their private clinics, which in Dr. Monasterio's case was across town, about a 20-minute car ride away. As soon as they were situated, usually around 3 PM, they operated on patient after patient. Surgeries often lasted until 9 PM. Emerging from the operating room didn't signify the end of the workday. The doctors would start examining patients who had scheduled evening appointments. The last examination would end around 11 PM. Having fulfilled their hospital and private practice obligations, the doctors would go home and eat dinner. Once they finished dessert, their workday resumed. They would spend two or three hours reviewing manuscripts and research projects before going to bed. After three or four hours of sleep, a new workday would begin.

Chapter Six

"Fernando was the greatest prototype to me, but he wasn't alone in this lifestyle," says Dennis. To be a leader in the field, the surgeons really had little choice. "The hospital system paid their doctors so poorly, maybe a couple hundred dollars a month, so the plastic surgeons depended on their private practice for income. But the research and advances in plastic surgery are in the hospital system, so they had to do both." Dr. Monasterio concurs. "My hospital salary probably would not pay my gasoline I use to go there, it is symbolic."

Tagging along with Dr. Monasterio left an immeasurable impact on Dennis. "Frankly, when I think I work really hard, I remind myself that it's no harder than what they're doing in Mexico and, for most of their day, they're making no money. Fernando validated my work ethic and attention to detail. I wanted to be like this man. I admired his style, his bravado, his accomplishments, his joy of life, his ability to function on three hours of sleep. He is my hero."

Dennis also saw in Dr. Monasterio someone who not only worked very hard, but also learned from his work. "There is experience, and there is something I call thoughtful experience," explains Dennis. "Just because you do things year in and year out and have a lot of experience doesn't mean nearly as much than if you really pay attention to what you are do-ing, why something didn't go exactly the way you wanted it to and how you will do better next time. I'm sure it's in every field. It's like hitting golf balls off the driving range. It doesn't mean anything if you don't pay atten-tion to what you are doing. Fernando was very self-critical all the time."

With those lessons learned, Dennis and his family returned to Pitts-burgh. They established more permanent roots there by buying, not rent-ing, a townhouse in Squirrel Hill. That sense of permanence must have pleased Dr. White and the University of Pittsburgh, which at long last had a craniofacial surgeon.

Dennis certainly found himself very busy. "Even though it's a very rare disorder, one in about 15,000 births, they're often treated incomplete-ly, so I inherited a lot of problem cases," he says.

He felt he was up to the challenge. Nevertheless, he did decide to make a phone call. "I had already done some craniofacial cases," he says, "but this particular case was the most difficult, a combination of terrible nose and eyes apart." The call was to Dr. Monasterio. He agreed to assist Dennis on the surgery at Pittsburgh's Children's Hospital. They weren't alone in the operating room for the eight-hour surgery. Dennis scheduled the operation to coincide with the regional meeting of the Ohio Valley Society of Plastic Surgeons, where Dr. Monasterio could be a guest speaker.

Many of the surgeons participating in the meeting weren't content to merely hear him speak. Not only was the operating room filled to capacity, the operation was broadcast via closed circuit television. The surgery involved using a rib graft to make the young patient's head more symmetrical. Neither Dr. Monasterio nor Dr. Hurwitz disappointed the crowd. "It went very well," says Dr. Monasterio. "I saw the patient many years later at a meeting with Dennis, when he presented that case. It was interesting," he adds in a consultative manner, "because the graft overgrew, grew more than we expected, but that was corrected.

"I also remember the case distinctly, because we had people watching and I said, 'Dennis, let's do things different than they expect.'"

The surgery was so rare that there was no common way to proceed, but most viewing the surgery expected the surgeons to perform the graft by going through the mouth. Dr. Monasterio spontaneously considered a different approach. When he explained it to his protégé, as they stood in the operating room, the young surgeon said, "Fine."

"Instead of going through the mouth," explains Dr. Monasterio, "we opened through an area of the skull and pulled the graft into the tiny incision." The creativity generating the novel approach was what drew both men to plastic surgery and what both men relished about the field. "You find out that something can be done differently." And, in this case, it led to a better outcome.

There was another benefit in the approach for Dr. Monasterio. "It confused the maxillofacial surgeons who were watching."

Chapter Six

After the surgery, Drs. Monasterio and Hurwitz grabbed a bite to eat and then headed to an indoor tennis court for a couple sets of spirited play. Dennis had more than 20 years of youth on his side, so he won more games than he lost, but that didn't keep every point from being competitive.

On the drive back to the hotel, Dennis witnessed something he never saw during his months in Mexico. His mentor yawned. "Fernando, I finally got you," Dennis said. "It looks like you're tired." The two friends smiled.

The operation solidified Dennis's reputation as a craniofacial surgeon, though he continued to find himself having to confront oral surgeons who considered themselves qualified to do craniofacial surgery. "It was an uphill battle. I was forever fighting the university's dental school and their surgeons. It was the most unpleasant part of craniofacial surgery."

But it wasn't the only unpleasant part of the specialty. "I got discouraged with craniofacial surgery, because I thought it was an exceptionally risky surgery without getting the desired results from repeated operations. I didn't see that there was great, great impact. The end result was that they didn't look normal, not even close, as opposed to cleft lip and palate patients, where I can make a huge difference, save their lives, really."

Dennis had already begun to establish himself in cleft lip work and also in aesthetic surgery, and that was where he wanted to focus his career.

With regard to the aesthetic work often performed on his female patients—the facelifts, the nose jobs, the tummy tucks—he has never hesitated in justifying the specialty. "It's a special thrill and privilege for me to take attractive women to the next level, not only because of the sensual and visual results, but because of how it makes them feel. To take a pretty woman who lost some of her beauty through an accident or age and give her her beauty back, it's what most of the male world treasures, the idea of making a beautiful person happy, why we lavish women with jewels.

"Maybe I'm trapped in the world of beauty, but if I am, so be it. Our society revolves around beauty. We have to get off the idea that beauty is superficial. Beauty is just another asset for a person that makes them achievable in society, just like high ethics, honesty, hard work. I'm not saying one is better than the other, but we need to get less and less apologetic to seeking beauty in humans. Look at Fiddler on the Roof: 'Matchmaker, is she beautiful?' This is from religious people. 'Make my spouse beautiful!' We have a dichotomy of thinking in our society where most intellectuals denigrate beauty, but the secret wish for all parents is that their child marries someone who is as attractive as possible."

It was an unspoken wish of Dennis and Linda for Karen.

The Chase for Beauty

Chapter Seven

When life is good, we take so much of it for granted. Our careers. Our family. Our friends. Our health. When life is good, it goes by quickly. A decade can pass in what seems like a month, or a week, or even a day. When life is good, we don't give much thought to how quickly it can change.

Life was good for the Hurwitzes. Not perfect—but definitely good.

Dennis had the career he wanted. He hadn't ignored his interest in cleft lip and palate surgery. As director of plastic surgery at Pittsburgh's Montefiore Hospital, and in conjunction with being the University of Pittsburgh's first full-time plastic surgeon, he began building a national reputation in pediatric surgery by operating on young patients who were born with the cleft lip and palate birth defects. Without surgery, each of these newborns—with a grotesquely deformed upper lip and nose—are sentenced to a life of stares, of ridicule, of pity, and, in all likelihood, missed opportunities. Anything and everything they accomplish in life will depend on overcoming a first impression that is not unlike being freshly hit in the face with a baseball bat. With plastic surgery, though, they can have a chance in life that they weren't given at birth. There were not many more than a handful of surgeons regionally, including Dennis, who gave these young patients that chance. Although the financial incentive for plastic surgeons is to treat adults, Dennis made cleft lip and palate surgery one of his specialties. He believed that the power and importance of beauty knew no age barriers. Starting with his return from Mexico in 1977 and continuing throughout the 1980s, he treated about 1,200 children who had a cleft lip and palate. Judging from the before and after pictures, all were successes, some bordering on miracles. He amassed stacks of letters from forever grateful parents.

Even in 1984, when he left his position at Montefiore Hospital to establish a private practice that focused on adult cosmetic surgery, he continued to be one of the few plastic surgeons in the region who treated cleft lip and palate patients. He did so by maintaining his academic affiliation with the university.

Through that affiliation, he also provided training for incoming medical students, residents, and fellows in what he dubbed "surgical art." It's an art that Dennis describes, not through a textbook, but, rather, one on one, like he did for a medical student who was interviewing for a plastic surgeon trainee position.

"He told me," recalls Dennis, "that one of his hobbies is raising orchards."

"'Why do you do that?' I asked."

"Because they are beautiful."

"Describe to me what is beautiful about an orchard?"

"Well, they are really nice to look at."

"Tell me about orchard beauty. What's the difference between a beautiful orchard and a very beautiful orchard—is it color, sharp contrast of colors, the geometry of it, how the flower twists and turns?"

"It feels beautiful."

"You have to get past that. Sure, that's the end result of beauty, but if you're in the beauty business, you need to recognize the component parts of beauty, what attracts people to it—its rhythm, its symmetry, its lack of symmetry, its inquisitiveness, its reflection of human form. You should always be breaking beauty down; it's nice to get that visceral effect, but if you are going to be building beauty, whether it's art or plastic surgery, then you have to think of the component parts.

"A plastic surgeon doesn't start by saying, 'Well I'm going to cut up something.' I start from what I see. It's a three-part phenomenon—observation; mental imagery; creation. In its parallel to medicine, the surgeon as the observer must look at the component parts—the bone, the soft tissues, the organs like the breast or the nose— how it all fits, what's there. It's just like an artist who looks at a scene: What's wrong? What's broken? What's not right? Then, the surgeon, through mental imagery, must move or reshape the components in different ways, just like an artist painting a scene may remove a telephone poll and wires or change the lighting to make the scene more beautiful. Finally, the surgeon has to have the medical capabilities to make it happen—raise the tissue, cut the tissue, put it together in a new way that creates beauty in a way that is least intrusive and allows for the process of healing. That's surgical art."

As the 1980s flew by, it was an art that defined him as a surgeon and that consumed him as a person—to his colleagues, to his patients, to his family, to his friends. For Dennis, that was good, because his artistry, by all accounts, was exceptional.

His success was just part of the Hurwitz fairy tale. Linda, too, was loving life—personally and professionally. After Mexico, she seemed to have mastered what eludes so many women—the ideal balance between being a wife, mother, daughter, and professional. She made Dennis feel invincible when she stood by his side, and she enhanced her own self-esteem by forging her own career, first in teaching and then becoming an administrator of a small Jewish day school and, in 1988, becoming director of the Holocaust Center of Greater Pittsburgh. She also made friends. Lots of them. Some became more than friends; they became family in a city where the Hurwitzes had no family.

Mara Reuben actually met Linda in the fall of 1975, not too long after the Hurwitzes made their first Pittsburgh friends, the Wolshes. When the two preschool moms played bridge at the home of a mutual friend, they quickly learned they had children around the same age. The Reubens had a daughter who was a year older than Karen and a son who was the same age. "Her two kids and Karen were friends all through school," says Linda. "They were really close." So were the parents, starting with that bridge game.

Chapter Seven

"Bridge all of a sudden became nonessential to the afternoon," says Mara, "because Linda and I didn't stop talking. She said to me, 'You have to meet my husband.' I said, 'I'm so excited; I can't wait.' It is rare that a foursome clicks right away." But the Hurwitzes and Reubens did. "Linda and Dennis loved activity." So did the Reubens. They became good friends before Mexico and even closer friends afterward. That first winter back from Mexico, the Hurwitz clan would often meet the Reuben clan for something fun, like sledding down a neighborhood hill. Then, they would have hot chocolate in front of the fireplace at the Reuben's Squirrel Hill home.

"We just became very close to them," says Linda.

"I brought Linda and Dennis into our circle of friends," says Mara.

In that circle of friends were Roz and Sandy Neiman, who had a daughter who was just two years older than Karen. Soon after Roz met Linda, she began making plans for their children to do things together. "We started going to the zoo, things like that," says Roz. The two moms quickly bonded, which meant introductions to the husbands couldn't be far behind.

Those hellos from Sandy Neiman, an attorney who graduated from Harvard University's law school, and from Dennis came at a get-together at another couple's home. Dennis was late, which was a shame because a doctor was suddenly needed. "Something flew into my eye," says Roz. "It was bad; I couldn't see." At last, Dennis walked in the door. Linda rushed him over to her new friend. "They threw me down on the floor," remembers Roz, "and he looked at me and said, 'Not bad, I'd just take a little off the chin.'

"That was the first thing he ever said to me. So, he got the thing out of my eye, and, from then on, we were inseparable."

By making friends, by getting involved in the Jewish community, and by establishing their careers, the Hurwitzes, in the blur of their life, had truly made Pittsburgh their home. Their commitment didn't go unnoticed by Dennis's younger sister, Marilyn. With a background in broadcast news, she found herself in a dead-end public relations position in Harrisburg a few years after graduating from college. When she decided to make a career move in 1979, it wasn't to her hometown of Baltimore.

"I looked in Pittsburgh," she says, "because I knew Dennis and Linda were there, and I wanted to at least have some family." Her job search was a success. A Pittsburgh radio station hired her as a reporter. "I was really excited I got that job; it was great."

She had another job, too, which came when she temporarily moved in with her brother and sister-in-law. "I lived with them for about a month until I found my own place, and, in return, I babysat for Karen; she was about seven years old." Marilyn got to know her niece very well.

There was an additional perk to living in the same city as Dennis and Linda. She had plenty of blind dates. "They really wanted me to get married, and so did I. They fixed me up with a lot of guys. Too many." One of the potential suitors, Dr. Joseph Turner, a physician specializing in otolaryngology, wasn't so bad. "The rest is history," says Marilyn about the young physician who would become her husband.

The Turners ended up living in Squirrel Hill. Unbeknownst to Linda, it was just a few blocks from her dream house. In 1984, after a Sunday brunch at the Turners, Dennis, Linda, and Karen decided to walk off the eggs and pastries by walking to a nearby open house. The three-story, five-bedroom home, originally built in 1897, had been updated to include a two-car garage, den, new kitchen, and new master bedroom. "When we walked through and saw the backyard, we just flipped," says Linda. Squirrel Hill isn't known for backyards, even among million-dollar homes. But this backyard had plenty of room for Dennis and Karen to throw a Frisbee or Linda and Dennis to host an outdoor dinner party.

Whether it was courting Linda, choosing a medical specialty, or sailing with Dr. Monasterio, Dennis was never passive. Linda knew he wouldn't let this home slip away from them. "We made an offer, and, very quickly, the owners came back with a counter offer. It was really close to what we offered and, we, literally within a day or two, agreed on a price. Then, we put our townhouse on the market ourselves and sold it and moved within a month."

It was a new way of life for Linda. "I never lived in an unattached dwelling," she says. "I always lived in a row house or half of a duplex or something. It was the kind of house I always wanted." It was certainly the kind of upscale, classic home that befitted a successful surgeon and his family.

Linda and Dennis had no reason to not like their lives, except for one regret. They had no luck having another baby. In 1984, Linda traveled to Philadelphia for an operation similar to the one she had in Pittsburgh. And, a few years later, there was a trip to an infertility clinic in Norfolk, Virginia, that specialized in vitro fertilization—removing eggs from the female's ovaries, fertilizing them with the male's sperm, and then placing the fertilized eggs in the woman's uterus with the hope that it will lead to a successful pregnancy. That hope never came to fruition for Dennis and Linda. It seemed more and more that Karen was destined to be an only child.

Such thoughts made Linda think back to a dinner she had in New York City in the early '80s while Dennis was there for a plastic surgeons meeting. Another plastic surgeon from Pittsburgh, Dr. William Schwartz, and his wife, Cindy, joined the Hurwitzes on the rainy night in Manhattan, and the two couples nonchalantly chose a Hungarian restaurant from among the seemingly endless number of dining choices.

Waiters weren't the only people weaving around the tables. A gypsy fortune-teller boldly approached diners to ask them if they wanted their palms read. When the gypsy reached Linda, she didn't refuse the entertaining offer. The gypsy, who looked very authentic in her Middle Ages garb, promptly took Linda's palm. She seemed to be doing more than just looking at the lines of Linda's hand as she apparently contemplated her client's fingers, skin, nails, and hand's shape. With the rain falling outside, the restaurant's central European atmosphere, and a gypsy who looked very much the part, Linda found herself thinking how real the moment seemed. She was excited to hear what good news was in her future.

The news was not all good. "She looked at me," says Linda, "and she said, 'You are going to have a catastrophic event in your early forties, and then you are going to have twins.'"

The revelation bothered Linda during dinner, after dinner, and when she returned home. "Her words haunted me," she says. "Then, when I couldn't have more kids, and went through all those in vitros, I kept thinking I'm going to get pregnant and have twins. It didn't happen. I just closed the door on that at 40. I finally said, 'Yeah, okay, I have to finally let go of it; we have one lovely child, and that is how it is going to be.'"

The year she let go was 1989—that first year of her early forties. Karen, meanwhile, was 17 years old. She was an honors student, worked part-time as a hostess at a local diner, and hoped to attend Boston University the following year and major in journalism or communication.

For some people, especially teenagers, that kind of thumbnail sketch would suffice. Not for Karen. "Karen was an unusual child," says Roz. "She was as sweet as any child you would want to meet, kind of shy, wasn't real social, but didn't have a mean bone in her body. I think Linda and Dennis kind of overshadowed her, because they were so social and so committed, and that can be a little daunting for a young girl. She was very sensitive. Very quiet."

Karen's grandmother, Mrs. Furst, also found that to be the case whenever she came to Pittsburgh to watch Karen when her parents were out of town. "With my other grandchildren, I am more strict. Somehow I never had a reason to be strict with Karen, because she was so vulnerable." In particular, she saw Karen's vulnerability first surface on the Avenue of the Dead in Mexico and, then, nearly 10 years later in Pittsburgh, when Dennis and Linda had gone abroad:

"Grandma, please sleep in my room," Karen pleaded to her grandmother when it was her bedtime.

Karen's grandfather wasn't pleased with the request. Karen was 14 years old at the time, so it seemed silly to him that she needed her grandmother to sleep in her room. "My husband was very upset, because we never slept apart," says Mrs. Furst. "But I said to him, 'I have to do this for Karen; she is so insecure, and my being in the room with her makes her more secure.'"

It was as if she was scared of some unknown evil. She even told her mother around this time about a dreadful, recurring premonition; she kept thinking someone was going to kill her on their home's back patio.

As Karen matured, though, her shyness and vulnerability began to give way to a heightened sensitivity, awareness of her surroundings, and introspection—traits that are often shared by authors and journalists. Mara noticed that correlation. "Karen was a brilliant writer," says Mara, who makes that assessment as more than just a friend of the Hurwitzes. Before earning a master's degree in communication from Chatham College in the mid-1980s, she had been assistant director of the honors program at the University of Pittsburgh when the program was founded in 1978. "The whole function of that honors program," she says, "was to create an oasis of quality in an urban setting and to recruit and retrain very bright, dynamic, highly motivated students. The honors students were groomed for prestigious fellowships and scholarships, not the least of which was the Rhodes Scholar. So, I have lots of experience working with admissions."

As the program's assistant director, she dealt with some of the brightest high school students in the country. Karen, in her assessment, was at that level. "She was a gifted writer. No question. She had the gift of conceptualization. An idea would take root, and, immediately upon taking root in her mind, the words would flow. Not only could she write prose, but she could write poetry equally as well. She was not articulate, she was not a talker, but she could think and express herself comfortably by writing. Writing was, in fact, her haven and her supportive climate, because nobody was there to judge—her perception mind you—within her world of writing. It was where the inside came outside."

The Chase for Beauty

In a high school essay titled *Ideals*, Karen wrote:

... The one thing I feel definite traces of is my bold, sort of romanticist ide-als. The funny thing is, a lot of people equate romantics with lost idealists, and really that is not it at all. Romantics are realists who grasp opportu-nities, take a couple risks ... go a little beyond what's secure and safe so that maybe they can end up with something special and a little out of the ordinary. These days, people are so set in being down to earth and on the straight and narrow, that they often block out or ignore something good or special because it might be dangerous. After all, people can turn on you, or expect total commitment, something might go wrong.... I learned that if I was gonna have some good things to say about my life, I'd have to take some risks.... I had a stronger, deep down determination to find something special.

*   *   **

In one way, Karen's contemplative nature demonstrated a depth far beyond her years; in another way, it made it difficult for her to fit in with some of her classmates. "She always had trouble with her peers," says Aunt Marilyn, "Growing up, whatever, she just seemed to not really fit in with mainstream. She just wasn't a popular kid, and that is how she ended up with friends that weren't mainstream, either."

Michale 'Mick' Anderson was one of those friends. "This was a down-and-out kid who sort of clung on to this little group Karen had of artsy, craftsy, writing, and drawing people," says Roz.

The childhood Mick portrays makes "down and out" seem like a huge understatement. Raised in a single-parent home, he showed signs at a very young age of being an academically gifted student. The Pittsburgh Public Schools placed him in its advanced studies program. When he was nine years old, he remembers bringing home a report card with straight A's. His mother wasn't there to greet him when he arrived. Instead, he says her boyfriend did so by holding him down for 40 minutes "and talk-ing shit to me." Afterward, he watched Bugs Bunny until he walked up-

Chapter Seven

stairs, where he says his mom's boyfriend was raping his twin sister. The boyfriend noticed Mick. "He beat me unconscious," says Mick. When he came to, he was given a warning: "If you tell your mom, I'll have sex with you." When his mom finally came home, her boyfriend was gone, and Mick says she was in a very bad mood. She didn't bother to look at the report cards. For no reason, Mick says she whipped him and his sister with an extension cord that left both of them with visible welts. Next, came a painful vinegar bath. In the bathtub, Mick says his mom noticed her daughter bleeding from the vagina, and she snapped out of her depression. She took them both to Children's Hospital and Mick says the moment the nurse saw the welt marks, she said to Mick's mom, "What the hell did you do to these kids?!"

The incident prompted Mick's maternal grandmother to get custody of the children, but Mick says abuse of varying degrees continued from his grandmother: "She pioneered the use of the extension cord." His grades started to slip. When he was in eighth grade, he returned to his mother's home, because she had married. He says he was "excited at first," but that changed when he found out his step-dad was a believer in corporal punishment. "He beat me with a belt," remembers Mick, after he had used some of his step-dad's work tools.

By then, he says, his grades had "flatlined." He didn't get kicked out of the public school's scholars program, though. Mick—who is African American—believes the system allowed him to remain in the program in order to maintain minority participation.

He says it wasn't that unusual for him to run away or get kicked out of the house by his mom. He always came back until the next time. "The only support I had," he says, "was with my friends." In the summer of 1988, that support wasn't enough. He slashed his wrists in an apparent suicide attempt. "I started carving on my arms," he says. "I don't know why. I was painfully sad." The attempt led to 30 days in a psychiatric ward at a local hospital, what Mick calls a "rubber room" where he was diagnosed with "clinical depression" and prescribed medication. "Mom tried to give me drugs," says Mick, "but I cussed her out and stopped."

The Chase for Beauty

Somehow, in spite of this physical and emotional turmoil, Mick could be a very gregarious individual. He had numerous friends that transcended all social boundaries. "I can't remember a time I didn't have friends," he says. "People were drawn to me." Also, he was a talented writer despite his declining academics. In 1988, he won a Pennsylvania Scholastic Press Association award for poetry, and he was recognized by the school board for his contributions in Peabody High School's magazine, *Beyond*.

Mick says he remembers meeting Karen by coincidence on the streets of Squirrel Hill in 1986, while he was walking with a friend who took a Jewish studies class with Karen. By chance, Mick and Karen bumped into each other again in the shopping district a few days later, and Karen invited him over to her home, which was just a few blocks away. Mick remembers her playing for him her favorite music: "The Beatles, the Doors, the Stones—classic rock. I said to her, 'Let it go, it's 20 years ago', but she just put on the Beatles' *Ob-La-Di, Ob-La-Da, Life Goes On*, dancing around happy." Mick liked her spirit. They became friends.

"I know I was her best friend," notes Mick. "I know I was her best friend, because she said and did things when I was around that she never did when I wasn't. I mean, looking back, she went to a Christian dance just to be with me."

Their relationship, he points out, was platonic but physical. "Karen was a hugger because our meeting routine involved these long 'soul-hugs' that could last minutes. Obviously, at a dance, it kinda made me feel awkward. Oh, I loved it on a personal level, but there were, like, girls there, you know? I'm trying to get out there and mingle, and I've got this chick hugging me unconscious in the middle of the dance floor. Funny. Point is that she didn't actually do that to other people. It was our thing."

Another one of their things, says Mick, was late, late night telephone calls. "It became our time. We talked about what we liked, what we didn't like. We talked until we fell asleep."

It didn't bother Karen that Mick was black, that he had an abusive childhood, and that he didn't have wealthy means. She saw nothing wrong with embracing those who are different. She saw the world as one, just as John Lennon did in Karen's favorite song: *Imagine*.

The legendary singer-songwriter's vision of an age when there would be no enemies, no prejudices, no killing is a future that Dennis—like most parents—wished for, too. That didn't mean he and Linda weren't concerned about some of Karen's friends, but both of them trusted her judgment, and they admired her understanding, compassion, and tolerance.

"One of my jobs was to drive Karen to school," says Dennis. "We would talk; it was brief, but I remember that. That was our special time." They would talk about life, about friendships. It came as no surprise to Dennis that Mick considered Karen her best friend, even though he knew that wasn't the case. "I think," says Dennis, "that Mick was really confusing 'the best person he knows' with who was 'his best friend.' He put her at the highest level."

So did Dennis. He was impressed with the person she was becoming.

At the start of her senior year in high school, Karen told her parents about her love for writing, something Dennis relished in high school, too. And she told them about her aspirations for the following year—to enroll at Boston University. Her dad couldn't help but notice her growing self-confidence and the substance of her future plans.

Mara noticed it, too. "Her shift was more a growth toward self, and her writings certainly reflect that. Karen was an old soul. A very old soul."

Linda asked Mara, with her communication background, to make sure Karen did everything necessary to be accepted to Boston University. Just like an aunt, Mara gladly helped out.

"I actually saw Karen for an intense, extended period of time, prepping her for her college interview at Boston University. We talked a lot about her college essay and what that meant to her and where that came from." For the essay, Karen, in part, wrote:

... An activity that I was involved in, which had a great influence on my social and political awareness, was the small, local youth group called

Youth Cry. Youth Cry is a local group of teenagers who meet to discuss world issues that are current and conflicting. We try to obtain information and speakers which represent all sides of the topics we think are important, and, in this way, we learn about events occurring around us that either directly or indirectly affect us and the society we live in.

Through Youth Cry, I can become directly involved and informed about issues that interest me and surround me. I have learned about and researched issues of abortion, the Contras of Nicaragua, the homeless, the hungry, apartheid in South Africa, and more.

With the narrowness of a teenager's lifestyle—often inclusive to only school related or trivial social activities such as clothes shopping or new movies—I can now broaden my scope of knowledge and gain real satisfaction in avid discussions and forums on wide ranges of worldwide topics…

Mara was impressed with the breadth and depth of Karen's humanitarian interests: "Karen had the ability to see the world through many different filters and to be able to express, in writing, her perspective, her insight, through those different filters. She did not see the world in just one way and was rather captivated by turning ideas inside out and upside down."

After reading Karen's essay and role playing with her, Mara had just one lingering concern. Normally, it would have been a parental concern, but Linda and Dennis were already in Boston for a conference, so Mara was in charge of putting Karen on the plane for her college interview in Boston. That meant she was the one who had to address the parental concern:

"I said to Karen, 'Now we have to decide what you are going to wear for the interview.' Her mom always dressed well and in an appropriate way. Karen couldn't have cared less. She was very devoted at that time in her life to sneakers. No matter what kind of attire she had on, she wanted to wear her sneakers."

Chapter Seven

"You cannot wear your sneakers to the interview; it is out of the question," Mara told Karen.

"No, I have to wear my sneakers. It makes me so comfortable."

"Part of being grown up—and being able to project yourself and who you are and, most importantly, who you are going to become through your education—is being able to present yourself properly. Karen, it is no different than presenting yourself in writing. There can't be any further discussion about it. We both know what is in your closet; so let's pick what is right and what shoes are going to go with it."

Back and forth the conversation went. Mara held firm until Karen proposed a compromise.

"I'm wearing my sneakers on the plane, and, even when my parents pick me up, I'm going to have my sneakers on, but I'll change into shoes for the interview."

"I'm going to hold you to this," Mara said. "You are wearing the shoes."

True to her word, Karen wore her sneakers during the flight to Boston. Her mom understood why. "She still wasn't totally comfortable with the fact that really she was a young woman who had a very lovely figure. She could have looked much more sophisticated but wasn't ready to step into that yet. She still liked to wear T-shirts and jeans."

But there was no denying that Karen was becoming a beautiful young woman, much like a butterfly coming out of a cocoon. Gone were the braces. Also gone were her glasses, thanks to a growth spurt around the age of 12 that reshaped her eyes, giving her 20/20 vision. Her hair seemed to be getting fuller, richer, and prettier, too, with the kind of natural waves and body that hairdressers are often asked to create. And, not too long into her teenage years, it became evident that she inherited her mom's sensuous figure. From a quick glance, though, she was an uncanny blend of both parents.

Her father, who made beauty for a living, noticed her transformation. "She was getting more and more beautiful, a natural beauty. She wore little makeup and was unpretentious, but she had a radiance about her." Her dad was a sucker for her angelic, fair complexion, her brown eyes that were always opened wide and seemed so full of love, and her face that had both a radiance and childlike innocence. More than anything, her dad took notice of her posture, always standing tall, all 5' 5" inches of her, as if she was showing the world that she was comfortable being Karen Hurwitz.

"She really was lovely," says her mom.

For the college interview, Karen, wearing shoes, didn't disappoint in either her appearance or in the substance of her remarks about life and helping people. "When she got in the car afterwards, she was so excited," says Linda.

Karen was growing up. Just a month earlier, in September of 1989, Roz also had a taste of Karen's burgeoning independence. She and Sandy took their two children and Karen to a Rolling Stones concert at Three Rivers Stadium. Just as they were getting situated in their field-level seats, Roz looked around, and Karen was not there.

"I went crazy." She was somewhere among 50,000 faces. After searching the entire field level, Roz found her surrogate niece hanging out with some friends behind the stage.

Like any aunt would do, "I grabbed her by the neck and said, 'Don't you ever do that to me again. If I don't return you to your parents in one piece tonight, they will kill, so sit there and don't move.'"

Afterward, Roz realized the young girl she knew since preschool was no longer a child. "She was just getting a sense of herself and a sense of her worth. She would never have gone off on her own before. She was a little scrawny girl, but now she was tall and built well and caring about her hair and, in fact, not long after the concert, I saw her shopping in the Gap. She had a pile of clothes":

"My mom is going to kill me."

Chapter Seven

"Your mom is not going to kill you; your mom is going to be so happy that you finally care how you look. If you don't charge it to Mom, charge it to me."

Roz called Linda to tell her that her baby girl was coming into her own. "It isn't that she wasn't anything before; she was just a shy little girl. Now, she was blossoming. She was a late bloomer." While this observation came from a dear friend of the Hurwitzes, it also came from a former schoolteacher who in 1986 switched careers into residential real estate sales and would amass approximately $230 million in sales during the next 20 years. Roz understood what it took to be successful, both in the classroom and in a career. So, when she told Linda and Dennis that Karen would one day make them proud, it was the kind of accolade that every parent wants to hear and every parent wants to believe.

Until October 27, 1989, the future for the Hurwitzes, all of them, seemed so perfect.

Chapter Eight

Friday, October 27, 1989, is not an easy day to explain. Not to the Hurwitzes. Not to their family, not to their friends, not to their community. Perhaps the best explanation of the day is to describe what it was not.

Friday, October 27, 1989, was not a day of beauty.

The day begins in peace for the Hurwitzes. At midnight, Dennis, Linda, Karen, and their visiting exchange student are at home. In bed. Asleep. Home security system on. Nothing out of the ordinary. An hour or so later, the telephone rings in Karen's room. She has her own line, so the ring isn't heard throughout the house. But is it heard on the Avenue of the Dead? By a gypsy in Manhattan? By the soul of Karen's great aunt who perished in the Holocaust? By Karen Hansen Clement?

Karen answers. The caller is Mick. That shouldn't have surprised Karen. "Our time" is what Mick had called these hours when most of the city sleeps. Except this time Mick doesn't want to talk on the telephone. He wants to see Karen.

Unlike his friend, Mick's future seems to be in turmoil, starting with his love life. He had a girlfriend who that fall enrolled at Allegheny College, which is about an hour's drive from Pittsburgh. When Mick recently went to pay her a visit, "she broke up with me." He had another potential girlfriend, the girl he calls "the love of my life"—who happened to be the mutual friend that introduced him to Karen. But she had just started a serious relationship with someone she met through Karen. That wasn't the end of his string of heartbreaks. A few weeks ago, he met at a party an Asian coed who attended Chatham College, located just a few minutes from the Hurwitz home. She seemed to fall for Mick's charm. He decided to pay her a visit earlier in the evening, only to find out, he says, that her dad, who was of Asian descent, forbid her to date a black man.

As for Karen, Mick even had recent issues with her. Late in the summer, she couldn't find her wallet that held her credit cards and bank debit card. Mick happened to be with Karen at her home when her wallet disappeared. "I reported the theft to the bank," says Linda. Bank officials began the tedious process of sifting through ATM machine surveillance photos. "We were waiting for any pictures that may have clarified someone trying to use Karen's card." Linda didn't really need to see the photos, though. She reasoned that, logistically, only Mick could have taken the wallet. Dennis concurred.

Mick sensed the suspicions of Karen's parents. "After a while," notes Mick, "it became clear that they [Dennis and Linda] considered me Suspect Number One." He says he was "pissed off at the Hurwtizes and Karen" and backed off seeing Karen for a few weeks.

School offered him no relief from his trouble with women. By the last week of October, his grades were so bad that he says his mom decided to withdraw him, so he could enter a job corps program and learn a skill. Mick wanted to be an English teacher, but with his academic record, he would have been hard pressed to graduate from high school, so a college education and teaching certification appeared highly unlikely. He went to school and pleaded with some of the administrators to reinstate him. "I was in tears," he says. "All my friends were there." School officials guaranteed nothing, but said they would consider his request. His mom, says Mick, wasn't as accommodating. Frustrated with her son's behavior, she kicked him out of the house.

Mick—out of school, unloved, and unemployed—found himself living on the street, with a couple of duffel bags of belongings, trying to survive by relying on friends. One of those friends was Karen. A few days before October 27, he got together with Karen and her family, the first time he had seen Karen or her parents since Karen's wallet disappeared.

The Hurwitzes hadn't yet informed the police of their suspicions about Mick. "I told Karen," says Linda, "that I thought he did it, but she said, 'If he did, he must really need it; I don't want to prosecute him.' I was torn. I didn't know what to do." So, she had him for dinner.

After they were done eating, Karen sought out her mother. "Karen asked if he could stay here," recalls Linda. "I said, 'No. His problems are too serious. He needs more help than we can offer.'" It wasn't the first time Linda made that assessment to Karen. In the summer of 1988, when Mick slashed his wrists, Karen was in the midst of a nationwide sight-seeing tour for high school students. She learned of Mick's plight from a letter sent to her by one of her friends. The news prompted her to write her mother.

"She couldn't comprehend that Mick would try to kill himself," says Linda. "She was so disturbed that someone would try to do that. How could someone be that upset? I said he's had a very disturbed family life, and even though he is smart and sensitive, something must have happened that gave him a bad sense of himself, made him so despondent. I wrote to her that his problems are more serious than you can solve."

More than a year later, with Mick's problems obviously not resolved, Linda tried to help him. Through her position at the Holocaust Center of Greater Pittsburgh, she knew some leaders of the Urban League of Pittsburgh, which is devoted to empowering African Americans to enter the economic and social mainstream community in Pittsburgh. There, he could talk with other black men who had difficult, fatherless childhoods. "I urged him to set up a meeting," says Linda. "I was trying to offer some alternatives, to help him see a future. I even said to him, 'You know, Mick, you are getting old enough that whatever happened with you and your mother and family, let go of it, don't let it destroy you. Decide what you want to do with your life.'"

Mick recalls the offer to help. "Mrs. Hurwitz says she knew prominent blacks in the community, she could've reached out to help me if I'd asked. With no offense intended, I was a kid; why would anyone need my permission to help me? Why would these folks be the logical choice anyway?"

Chapter Eight

Instead, he chose to stay on the streets, and, on Thursday, October 26, Mick and his duffel bags had nowhere to go.

Not so for the Hurwitzes. Earlier in the day, Dennis put in his usual long hours at the hospital while Linda had a board meeting dealing with Black-Jewish dialogue, regarding how the two groups could improve their relations. That evening, Dennis and Linda attended a monthly Jewish studies class. The session dealt with the importance of children respecting their fathers and mothers and why it is one of the 10 Commandments.

Karen, after her day at school, had a more entertaining evening. She went with a girlfriend and her family's visiting exchange student to her high school's football game. When the parents and daughter reunited at home just before the 11 o'clock news, Dennis says, "Karen plopped down next to me in a big recliner chair." The recliner wasn't meant for two people, but Dennis didn't mind. "Somehow, there was enough room. It felt just right. She gave me a hug; nothing special, but it was nice. We said goodnight and went to sleep."

While they slept, Mick wound up at a pay phone outside the Squirrel Hill library, not far from where he first met Karen. There was no one to meet on the streets now. They were deserted.

The destiny of October 26 had passed and the destiny of October 27 was about to begin as Mick picks up the phone and makes the call.

"Can you come meet?" Mick asks. He says he wants to talk about their future. He remembers Karen's groggy response:

"No. Do you know what time it is? I'll see you tomorrow. Are you okay?"

"No," Mick says, and he starts to cry. "Everything is going wrong."

Mick says the conversation about his plight continued until he finally asks:

"Do you mind if I come over?"

He says Karen agrees: "Well, it's really late, but, okay, I'll meet you."

Mick grabs his duffel bags and makes the five-minute walk to the Hurwitz home. He says he went to the back of the house, drops his duffel bags on the patio table, and, as Karen instructed, waits for her to open the back door off of the patio.

Inside the home, Karen turns off the security system, causing the keypad in the master bedroom to beep for a moment. Like most dads, Dennis hears nothing; like most moms, Linda wakes up. She quietly calls out to Karen, asking her if she is all right:

"Yeah, I can't sleep. I'm going downstairs for some cookies and milk."

"Do you want me to come with you?" asks her mom.

"No, don't worry about me; I'm okay," answers Karen.

Normally, Linda would keep her daughter company anyway. She always had in the past. But, tonight, for some unexplained reason, she doesn't. Even more uncharacteristic for her is that she quickly falls asleep again.

Karen goes downstairs, and, while holding her poodle, Pooh, in her arms, she opens the back door. She gives Mick a hug, but Pooh, isn't as pleased to see the visitor. "He yipped at me," Mick says. Karen guides her guest to the dining room, where he says they sat down and talked awhile, and where Karen, over a glass of milk, gives him some advice:

"Make me a promise, that you're going to try and get your grades up. You're messing your life up."

"I told her I knew I had to buckle down," Mick says, and he tells her what that means for the two of them: "I can't hang out and have fun, too many distractions."

Karen is understanding, says Mick, mentioning that she is getting busier, too, with school and college planning.

They keep talking.

"She asked me to be quieter," says Mick. She feared waking her parents. But she had no fear of Mick. Both agree the time has come for Mick

Chapter Eight

to leave. He says she walked him out the back way where, just outside the patio door, he stumbles over one of his bags.

"I have something for you," he says. He wants to give her a set of nunchucks, a martial arts weapon that consists of two sticks connected at their ends with a short rope. It's not a typical present, but Mick says he gave the same gift to a few girls he knew, so they would have a self-defense weapon in case they were ever assaulted. To find the present, he has to pull out of his bag a samurai sword.

While he keeps searching for the nunchucks somewhere in his duffel bag, he says Karen keeps talking about "me rebuilding my life, her going to college."

That is the last of his conversation with Karen he says he remembers before he turned October 27, 1989, into a day of unimaginable ugliness.

"I reached down, grabbed the sword, I stabbed her," he says.

Linda is jarred from her sleep once again. She hears the garage door going up. It's nearly 2:30 in the morning. She is confused. Lying in bed for a moment, not fully awake, she tries to make sense of what is happening. She can't. She doesn't nudge Dennis, though, because she knows he will be upset with Karen if he finds out she went for a drive in the middle of the night. Maybe, she hopes, Karen will have a plausible explanation. Perhaps she took a friend home who, for whatever reason, stopped by very late while Karen was having her cookies and milk.

With Dennis still sleeping, she gets out of bed and goes downstairs in her nightgown. The garage door is still open. The car is still gone. She realizes she can't figure this out by herself, so she hurriedly goes back upstairs and awakens Dennis. Together, they are bewildered. Neither knows what to do. Dennis wonders if they should call the police. Linda, now fully awake, slips into her robe and slippers and goes downstairs once more, searching for some clue about what has happened. She finds it. Karen's wallet with her driver's license is in the house. "Karen was a new enough driver that she wouldn't have done that, even to drive a couple of blocks," says Linda. Then, Linda notices something else. Pooh is outside barking, and the back door is open. She turns on the patio lights and walks outside.

"She's here! She's here!"

Dennis, barefoot and in his pajamas, runs outside. Onto the patio. Into a nightmare. "It was pretty dim, but I could see her." His daughter is lying between the bushes bordering the patio. "I was immediately aware she was motionless, lying on her back."

There is some light coming from somewhere, he's not sure where, maybe a neighbor's porch light or a distant street light. Wherever the light is coming from, it seems to illuminate Karen's face, though her brown eyes, always so full of love, are undeniably different. "All I sort of saw was an open-eye, blank stare, and her mouth was wide open."

He and Linda see some streaks of blood, too. On their daughter's face. In her hair. On her sweatshirt. The accomplished surgeon does the only thing he can at this point. He howls into the night. A howl of disbelief, of anger, of sorrow, and, most of all, of pain. It is an animalistic howl that shakes the soul of Linda.

Neither parent accepts what they see. Linda, in hysterics, goes inside and calls 9-1-1. She must get help. Dennis stays at his daughter's side, trying to think like a doctor. He places his hand on Karen's neck. "She was already slightly cool to the touch." He feels and feels and feels for the steady beat in the carotid artery. It can't be found. He convinces himself that it's his anxiety as a parent, not her condition, that accounts for his inability to find a pulse.

"Still touching her neck, I positioned my ear to her nose and mouth expecting to hear and feel the sweet light puffs of exhalation air." He hears and feels nothing. "My heart sank deep in desperation." He knows.

"Maybe I'm wrong," he prays as his wife tells him that the paramedics are on the way. He won't give up. "I tried to put breath back in her and pump her chest to circulate her blood until help could come and tell me that I was wrong and all would be well."

Chapter Eight

He tries not to contemplate the significance of what looks like a deep wound to her heart. When he, then Linda, breathe for her, by giving her mouth-to-mouth resuscitation, the air escapes though the wound. And the chest compressions only bring blood to her mouth. Still, with his wife watching over him, Dennis doesn't stop. He continues to do all he medically can for "my breathless, beautiful child." While he does so, he wails over and over again into the darkened sky, "My baby's gone! My baby's gone!"

Help finally arrives in about 15 minutes. By then, Dennis is hoarse. Linda is numb. Karen is still dead.

Chapter Nine

For the Hurwitzes, sleep is no longer part of October 27, 1989's predawn hours. It has been replaced by confusion. Horror. Anger. Sorrow. Police questioning.

Ron Freedman, the commander of Major Crimes of the Pittsburgh Police, is at the Hurwitz home not much later than the paramedics. "When a 9-1-1 call would come in like this call," says Detective Freedman, "I was alerted automatically. This happened early in the morning. I was alerted, it was not far from where I lived, so I just got up, brushed my teeth, dressed, and was out the door. I responded very quickly. That was my policy, to go to as many homicides as I could."

Freedman, who spent nearly 20 years as a homicide detective and almost 15 more years as commander, had seen his share of homicide crimes. But, he says, he never saw anything quite like what happened to Karen.

Karen's father, who had to be pulled away from his daughter when the paramedics arrived, uses one word to describe what happened: "Barbaric." Detective Freedman doesn't disagree. His homicide detectives call it one of the most vicious stabbings they have ever seen.

Karen is pronounced dead at the scene. It's the detectives' job to find out what happened. Detective Freedman makes some quick decisions. First, he deduces that the killer knew Karen.

"If this had been a stranger abduction," he says, "what is the likelihood of the perpetrator getting into this home that is locked and alarmed and getting the victim out of the house with her parents sleeping there?"

Since no forced break-in could be detected, the detectives have to consider those in the home. "Do we suspect the family? Had we not resolved this thing, we would have looked at them very closely," says Detective

Freedman, "but to make a quick assessment, this wasn't the family. This is not the kind of murder you see of a family member. Our quick assessment was that this is somebody who knows her, not a stranger, though you could be completely wrong. You always have to allow for that."

If the murderer wasn't a stranger and it wasn't a family member, the detectives needed to identify anyone Karen knew who might be capable of such a killing. Dennis and Linda didn't have a long list of names to supply the detectives, and that list became very short when nunchucks are found in the Hurwitz backyard. "I thought they might be Mick's," says Linda, "I knew he was into martial arts a little bit."

The moment the police locate his whereabouts, they will bring him in for questioning. The case had immediate priority.

"It isn't that one life has more or less value," says Detective Freedman, "but Karen Hurwitz was not a drug dealer. She was not a prostitute. She wasn't a gang member. Here is a young lady who is asleep in her bed, in her own home, and suddenly she is murdered very violently. So, you look at that, and it is the kind of case that affects you in a way that some cases don't. Right or wrong, that is the reality of it."

Detective Freedman doesn't just feel badly for the victim. He pities the parents. "When we were working, I watched Dennis, and he was just about to explode. I felt so sorry for him. I put myself in his position, and I thought, 'Could I even begin to function the way he is functioning?' I have three daughters. If I found one of my daughters in that condition, I would just want to run away. So, I said to him, 'Let's take a walk.' He and I walked and walked and walked. It was good for both of us. It really was. We walked through the neighborhood and just talked."

The walk takes them to the home of Dennis's sister, Marilyn. Detective Freedman rings the doorbell. Marilyn comes to the door; it's 3 AM. Marilyn says her brother looked like he was in shock. Detective Freedman did the talking. By the time they left, Marilyn says she was no longer Jewish. "I was mad. I was so angry at God. That is what convinced me that it was a mistake to believe in God. I know things have happened to other people, too; where was God for that? There are a lot of people that believe in God like my brother Shimon; I can't see how they can. I think that everything is random. They are more forgiving of God, I think, than I am."

After the conversation ends, Marilyn wants to "curl up and die." She doesn't. Her sister-in-law needs her. Linda, still at home, is distraught that she can't go to her backyard anymore. It is a crime scene. "I couldn't stand that," she says. "I couldn't go back out there and just sort of say goodbye again."

Dennis's walk with Detective Freedman continues. He shares intimate facets of his daughter's life with a man who was a stranger to him when the night began. "He told me a lot of things," says Detective Freedman. "Like anybody else that is raising a teenage daughter, they do things that you don't like them doing, but you give some free rein, let them find themselves, express themselves, and he was telling me things he liked about her, and things he wished she wouldn't have done.

"I had to ask him, was she having sex with somebody? Was she cheating? Was she stealing? Was she doing drugs? I need to ask all of those things, and here is a person—a man who just lost his daughter whom he loved dearly—and he has someone asking, 'Is your daughter a junkie?' To me that is the hardest thing, to ask somebody those question. But I had to. He understood."

Too many times, says Detective Freedman, the loved ones of crime victims don't grasp the urgency for immediately sharing all they can with detectives. They are simply too overwhelmed with grief to think rationally. Not so with the Hurwitzes. Despite the shock and horror they just endured, they hold nothing back all night long, continuing to answer question after question. "We were just trying to be helpful," says Dennis. In their minds, they had no other choice. They wanted the case solved.

The eternally long night finally comes to an end. The sun rises. Just another Friday for Mara Reuben in Squirrel Hill, who is in her kitchen having a cup of coffee before leaving for work. Her plans for the day suddenly change when her son, Gregg, who was Karen's classmate, unexpectedly bursts through the door. On his way to school, he had passed the Hurwitz home. It was surrounded by police cars. Instead of going to school, he hurried home.

"When he walked in the door, he grabbed my hand with the coffee and said something happened at the Hurwitzes. He was so distraught," says Mara. After the coffee splatters on the floor, Gregg reaches out to his mom and they hug. Mara wants to console her son, but all she can think about is the Hurwitzes. "Greggy, go back to school if you can," Mara tells him. "I'm going to Linda's."

Gregg feels too stunned to go back to school, but his mom has no more time to comfort him. She breaks off their hug knowing that her son understands. The Hurwitzes were in some kind of trouble, and Mara has to be there for them. "I went right over," she says. "We were like family."

At the Neimans, Sandy, is an early riser. He often writes his legal papers while the rest of the household is asleep. But on Friday, October 27, his predawn routine is interrupted by an early morning errand. His son, Noah, has a preschool picnic later in the day and needs a packed lunch. There is no bread or peanut butter in the house, so Sandy must drive to a nearby supermarket. Before he goes, he unplugs the bedroom telephone to make sure Roz won't be disturbed by some rude real estate agent calling before sunrise.

Sure enough, while he's gone, the phone rings. A few minutes later it rings again. Then again. The repeated rings throughout the house awaken Roz, but she is still in a sleepy haze and can't plug in the bedroom phone in time to find out who is calling. The incessant ringing makes her grumpy. "Who in the world keeps calling at this hour?" she angrily wonders.

In the next moment, the rings become inconsequential. "I heard the most blood-curdling scream I ever heard in my life." The alarming cry emanates from her husband. "The only thing I could think of was there had been a nuclear war," says Roz. "I ran to Noah's bedroom to make sure he was okay." He was fine, sound asleep. Her husband was not. "Sandy kept screaming, and he was crawling up the steps on his hands and knees.

Suddenly, his screams became coherent. "Karen is dead!" He heard it in the car on a radio news station while on the way to the supermarket. He never bought the peanut butter or the loaf of bread. Sandy and Roz, in tears, embrace. Then, the phone rings again, but they don't answer.

"We just jumped in the car and went over there."

"When I walked in," says Roz, "Linda looked at me as cold and as dead pan as you could imagine, and she said, 'I'm not a parent anymore.' Then, Dennis grabbed me and collapsed. He looked at me and said, 'I will not go through the next 30 years childless.' Those were his first words to me."

When Mara arrives, she, too, learns the grim news. "Linda was holding my hand, we were sitting on the sofa, and she told me exactly what happened, hearing the noise, going downstairs, and then going outside, finding Karen, trying to give her CPR, and her lips were still warm. I thought I would die, and I believe that a piece of me died right then. Linda was still retelling the event, trying to have it make sense when you can't make sense of anything."

Marilyn and some other friends had already congregated at the Hurwitzes. A few stayed out front, talking with the police, keeping the press away. Some kept busy cleaning the house. Others held hands and wept.

"Our friends created like a cocoon around us," says Linda, "It was amazing, really wonderful." Still, none could ease their pain. For Linda, the only one who comes close is her mother. She had dreaded making the telephone call to her parents, both Holocaust survivors. How much tragedy can two people endure in a lifetime? When her dad answers the phone, she can't tell someone who had already lost his first wife and children in the Holocaust that his granddaughter had just been murdered. She can only say, "I want to talk to Mom." Somehow she finds the courage to tell her mother what happened. Her mother's first words are: "No one will ever really be able to help you, but you will get through it."

Those words never leave Linda's mind. "I kept saying that to myself, 'You'll get through it.'"

Chapter Nine

Dennis has another thought that wouldn't go away. "I'm not a dad anymore."

He, too, has trouble telling his family. Marilyn helps by calling some of their family, including their parents and their brother, Bill. No matter who finds out what happened—parent, brother, relative, friend, stranger—the reaction is the same; it's one of shock, anger, and mourning. Bill, who lives with his wife and two school-age sons in New Jersey, is already at work when he learns of Karen's fate. He immediately calls his wife, Ivy, and within a few hours, his family is on a flight to Pittsburgh. When they arrive at the Pittsburgh airport and rent a car, the agent behind the desk looks at the last name and asks, "Are you the family whose daughter was murdered?" Looks of despair provide her with the answer.

Dennis's divorced parents travel to Pittsburgh, too—his dad coming from Baltimore and his mom from California. The one family member who isn't traveling to Pittsburgh is Dennis's brother, Shimon. Western culture and Jewish culture are too different, says the oldest child. He thinks his beliefs may cause more pain than comfort. He may be right.

Dennis remembers his brother saying that perhaps Karen's death is a message from God that Dennis needed to be more Jewish. Shimon knows that response can seem harsh, even cruel. But it is truly what he believes, "Most people," he says, "will just think it is bad luck or the way the cookie crumbled. Dennis has a Creator; he has to figure out what his Creator is trying to tell him. If he doesn't figure it out, one day hopefully it will be clear. I think all of us have to do that in our lives. The real question is how can such a wonderful person have anything go wrong at all? What is the Jewish take on these things? We have been through a lot. I live in Israel now; every day by the grace of God we don't have terribleness. The real question comes up over and over again. Why do such terrible things happen to good people? Why is it that we can be doing everything right and things go wrong? This is something that requires much more Jewish background. We try to help people understand this if they are interested."

He wants Dennis to be interested. Bill and Marilyn, too. "My whole work today is helping Jews get on board with their Judaism. That is all I do."

Dennis is not ready to become more religious. His faith is in turmoil. "My sister on one side is no longer Jewish, and my brother is saying God is telling me something." He thinks about Psalm 23, which is often chanted at Jewish funerals:

The Lord is my shepherd; I shall not want

He maketh me to lie down in green pastures; He leadeth me beside the still waters.

He restoreth my soul; He guideth me in straight paths for His name's sake.

Yea, though I walk through the valley of the shadow of death, I will fear no evil, for Thou art with me; Thy rod and Thy staff, they comfort me.

Thou preparest a table before me in the presence of mine enemies;

Thou hast anointed my head with oil; my cup runneth over.

Surely goodness and mercy shall follow me all the days of my life;

And I shall dwell in the house of the Lord forever.

"The inference is God is the one who will show us what evil is and protect us from it, because we can't do it ourselves. This is what we pray about," says Dennis. "We pray that evil will not strike us, but what is evil? Evil is not necessarily the recognized tyrants who enslaves and kills people. We ask God to protect us from evil, from that which we cannot see, from those who do things like this who we don't figure out. We think that maybe we are smart enough to stay away from known criminals and assassins, but we need protection from God from just this sort of thing. This is inexplicable. This is the evil that we need help from God. But God could not help on this occasion. Why? Well, the very religious, they tell us that we don't understand. There is a good reason, we just can't fathom it. Maybe we will figure out in our next life if there is such a thing. God knows why. But we have to go through all of this pain, and Karen had to lose her life. Maybe we didn't pray well enough to protect us from evil. To take it on a spiritual sense, this is what brings people to prayer, because we cannot protect ourselves from this. What do I take from this? That is the best I can do."

The best he can do isn't very satisfying to him: "If God is all powerful, and this is what God does, then I don't need that God."

Around noon, slightly more than nine hours after Karen's last breath was taken from her, Mick Anderson is arrested. He had retreated to a friend's home after the killing and agreed to surrender at Peabody High School once he learned police were looking for him. During interviews at police headquarters, Mick, with Karen's blood still on his clothes, confesses to the killing. He also tells police where he parked the Hurwitz's car, in Highland Park, an East End neighborhood adjoining Squirrel Hill. Detectives drive with Mick to retrieve the car and, after searching the area, they find the sword.

With the confession, the car's recovery, and the murder weapon, there is nothing left to do but to charge Mick with criminal homicide in the murder of Karen Hurwitz. "We feel it was premeditated," says Police Chief Ralph Pampena. "The investigation shows he went there with the intent to kill her." In addition, Mick also faces theft charges for taking the Hurwitz's automobile and for stealing Karen's wallet two months ago and using the credit cards to spend $600 of her money.

In Mick's written murder confession, he offers no motive other than stating he did "bad things" when he wore a T-shirt from the motion picture, *A Clockwork Orange.*

Linda vividly remembers the 1971 award-winning film. She was so repulsed by the movie's savagery that she walked out of the theater before it ended. She happened to be pregnant at the time with Karen.

The movie is director Stanley Kubrick's adaptation of Anthony Burgess's 1963 acclaimed novel of the same name. The main character, Alex,

The Chase for Beauty

is the leader of a gang of vicious hoodlums who spend their nights committing crimes that escalate into more and more violence, culminating in rape and murder. Alex is eventually caught and programmed to disavow violence. Ultimately, he is deprogrammed and set free, and it's implied that his devious ways will resume.

On January 9, 1972, *The New York Times* chief film critic Vincent Canby published his comments regarding the motion picture:

Stanley Kubrick's ninth film, "A Clockwork Orange" which has just won the New York Film Critics Award as the best film of 1971, is a brilliant and dangerous work....

"A Clockwork Orange" might correctly be called dangerous only if one doesn't respond to anything else in the film except the violence. One critic has suggested that Kubrick has attempted to estrange us from any identification with Alex's victims so that we can enjoy the rapes and the beatings. All I can say is that I did not feel any such enjoyment. I was shocked and sickened and moved by a stylized representation that never, for a minute, did I mistake for a literal representation of the real thing.

Everything about "A Clockwork Orange" is carefully designed to make this difference apparent, at least to the adult viewer, but there may be a very real problem when even such stylized representations are seen by immature audiences. That, however, is another subject entirely, and one for qualified psychiatrists to ponder....

Seventeen years later, that subject had onerous relevance in Pittsburgh and left Linda to wonder if part of her revulsion to the film was a "foreshadowing" of what was to come.

In Mick's accompanying 32-minute tape-recorded confession, he admits that he stabbed Karen with his samurai sword in the backyard just

Chapter Nine

after Karen told him how much she cared for him. He says they ended up in the backyard because Karen was worried about her parents coming down the steps. They had been talking about "each other, about the future, and just about anything." When they went outside, he says he started having "strange feelings" after touching his samurai sword. "I just wanted to be violent and I wanted to hurt myself, and I wanted to hurt anything else that was there."

It was a violence not unfamiliar to Linda, at least from a literary standpoint. In her 1972 mater's thesis about violence as a source of self-identity for the black male, she wrote:

In the short stories and novels of Richard Wright, one finds ideas that help understanding of the psyche of poor, oppressed people and the personalities and motivations of individuals under severely restricted ways of life. Wright shows, especially in Native Son *and "Big Boy Leaves Home," that in life a black boy has to suffer both in the North and the South. He makes the reader experience the poor physical conditions, the filth and squalor of tenements and farm huts, the degradation and inferiority bred and fed by whites. His stories involve one in the humiliation of being considered less than human, of feeling chained, restricted in every mode of living. After he has your emotional empathy for this torturous life, he reveals the freedom and elation that can be felt by a boy committing an aggressive action. Just because he has been unable to* do *or achieve anything in his life, the action, though violent and murderous is something accomplished by him and thus gives a sense of creation. Experiencing a free-willed action gives a sense of power; power gives an illusion of freedom and movement; this feeling is so new and pleasing that the actor is obsessed with it, not with the results of his deed.*

Since October 27, 1989, the premise of her thesis—or why she picked it for that matter—haunts Linda, but before that date neither she, nor evidently Karen, sensed this kind of *violent and murderous* rage in Mick.

In his confession to police detectives, he says Karen "insisted she cared about me. She closed her eyes and started to recount from the time I met her." It was then that Mick says he struck Karen on the top of the head with the sword, injuring her and causing her to scream. Her cries of "No, Micki, no!" momentarily awakened a neighbor nearly half a block away. To quiet her, Mick says he began choking her and knocked her to the ground. "I wanted to shut her up, because she kept screaming.... And I just wanted to get it over with, because it was already over with from the time I struck her."

But it wasn't over. In his confession, Mick describes wrestling and choking his good friend until she ceased to move. Once he let go, though, he says Karen sat up and asked him what he was doing. Mick didn't answer with words. Instead, he says he found his sword and stabbed. Again and again and again and again and again. "She still kept screaming. I fell beside her and started choking her and then she ceased movement." Evidently, she put up a valiant fight for her life. Detectives noted broken branches on nearby bushes and a patio flagstone shoved out of the ground.

The autopsy report concluded that Karen died from six thrusts into a single entry wound in the chest that passed though her heart and perforated her lungs. She was also manually strangled and suffered stab wounds on the cheek and behind the right ear. Her face and neck were bruised, and she had a three-inch cut and slight fracture on the top of her skull.

Neither the autopsy report nor Mick's written and taped confessions give a definitive motive. Perhaps Linda's thesis provides the best perspective on what happened. Although, Detective Freedman has his opinion based, not on anything Mick said directly to him, but just from the nature of the crime, Mick's background, and his knowledge of the case:

"I think it was nothing more than frustration and grief and him not having his way. He liked to be in control. He liked to dominate; he liked things done the way he wanted, and he realized that Karen had a lot of potential in terms of him getting material things from her—getting money—and he thought that the relationship was going in one direction and it wasn't."

Chapter Nine 101

Mick needed to be Karen's friend almost like she was a paycheck, an insurance policy, but Detective Freedman explains that Karen expected and deserved more from a friendship than simply being a benefactor.

"She realized—she talked to people, and we talked to people—and she realized she is planning to go off to college and he had stolen the money from her. This wasn't the kind of guy she wanted to be associated or linked with, and she knew she had to end the relationship, because she was going to go away, and he wanted to continue it in a romantic fashion. It wasn't because I think he was interested in her truly as someone that he liked or that he realized the relationship could develop and evolve into a love or something. He was just there looking to see what he could get, and she said no.

"He couldn't accept no. He talked to her on the phone, and I'm sure he probably said, 'I'll just see you one more time,' thinking that he could talk her into it, and when he couldn't, he killed her. Clearly, he took a weapon with him. It was probably to threaten her with, 'damn it, she better or whatever,' and then when she said no is no, he was not going to take no. He killed her for personal reasons. He didn't want somebody being in control. He wanted to be in control. His true personality came out; that is what it was. That is the kind of guy he is; violent, vicious, and a brutal son of a bitch."

Whatever Mick's motive, there can be no denying the end result. Karen's life came to an untimely, unjust, cruel end. For Dennis and Linda, their last memory was one of holding a broken, lifeless child. There would be no last look into her innocent eyes. Or so they thought.

Given the tragic circumstances, their Portugal exchange student, Marta Matos, would move in with another Pittsburgh family to complete her abroad studies. Just before changing addresses, she has some film developed that is filled with scenes of her life in Pittsburgh. There were so many snapshots taken at so many different times, she has no idea what would be handed to her at the store. When she picks up the stack, there is one photograph, in particular, that she doesn't remember taking.

The Chase for Beauty

It is of a young woman walking home from school. On a whim, her friend made her halt for a moment, so she could be caught on camera. The young woman stopped walking, but she didn't really pose. With one hand resting comfortably in her front pants pocket and the other casually holding the strap of her book bag, she looked confidently into the camera and smiled. It's not a forced smile. It's real, as real as the tree-lined street in the background, as the colorful fall leaves covering the branches, as the mid-October sunlight casting Picasso-like shadows on the ground. The young woman, standing tall, seems very comfortable with who she is, very much at peace with her world. The photo-snapping friend is Marta. The young woman is Karen.

When Marta gives Karen's parents the snapshot, their reaction is understandable. At first glance, Linda collapses. Dennis sobs.

"It was so profound," he says. "We knew that was her last picture. It was such a wonderful gift." Considering all that had happened, it is amazing that he could look at anything as a gift. But he did, and he took his gift to the camera store and ordered additional copies of the picture, which he and Linda placed everywhere—in their offices, in their bedroom, throughout their home.

"It's my Mona Lisa," says Linda.

The Chase for Beauty

Chapter Ten

Linda's Mona Lisa arrived a week after Karen's murder, so it wasn't present when the community offered its farewell. In Judaism, according to Deuteronomy, the deceased must be buried as soon as possible; the soul has returned to God, so the body shouldn't be left to linger in the land of the living. Burial can't take place on the Sabbath, though, the day of rest, which is from sundown Friday until sundown Saturday. In keeping with this tradition, Karen's funeral was scheduled for Sunday, October 29, at the Burton L. Hirsch funeral home in Squirrel Hill, just two days after she took her last breath.

Arrangements had to be made quickly. Dennis and Linda, functioning on very little sleep, found themselves choosing Karen's casket and making plans at the funeral home on the very same day she died. Burton Hirsch, the funeral director, did his best to be sympathetic. "We know your pain," the father of two, told Dennis and Linda. "Our son died, too." His empathy offered no solace to Dennis: "They still had one child, I lost a whole family. It was all gone. Everything. There was no more Mom and Dad. If you have more children, it must be better than having none. That may be self-centered, but it's real, and I'm not going to hide from that."

The senselessness of what happened gnawed at Dennis and Linda, too. "This was no murder mystery," says Linda. "Within a day, we knew who did it. We didn't know why. There was no why. That became obvious almost immediately. There was nothing that cold have justified this. Nothing!"

The senselessness seemed to bother everyone. Newscasters gave updates on the case with tear-filled eyes. "They could hardly get through their reports," says Dennis. The friends of the Hurwitzes were in far worse shape. "Our friends were just so traumatized," says Linda. "There was such a sense that if it happened to us, it can happen to anyone."

It seemed even their rabbi, Alvin Berkun of Tree of Life Congregation, didn't know what to say. "Nobody knew what to say," says Linda. "A horrible, horrible unfair thing happened. What can you say? There is nothing to say."

About 1,000 mourners attended the funeral. The crowd was so large that hundreds had to stand outside the funeral home. The city's morning newspaper, the *Pittsburgh Post-Gazette*, published a photograph on page one of the mourners lining the sidewalk. Mr. Hirsch, in an accompanying article, said that he hadn't seen such an outpouring of sympathy since the death of Allison Krause of Squirrel Hill. Ms. Krause was one of the four Kent State college students shot and killed by the Ohio national guardsman in May 1970 during a campus protest against the Vietnam War.

The mourners weren't just friends and acquaintances from Pittsburgh. Many of Dennis's medical colleagues were in attendance—some local, some coming from cities across the country.

One plastic surgeon not sitting in the pews was Oscar Ramirez, who is an assistant professor at Johns Hopkins University and the University of Maryland and who has a private practice in Baltimore. Dr. Ramirez first met Dr. Hurwitz when he completed his residency at the University of Pittsburgh. Dr. Hurwitz had been one of his teachers, and now they were peers, collaborating on papers and debating each other at national medical meetings. The debates, says Dr. Ramirez, weren't always for the faint of heart:

"I would present a paper or he would present a paper, and I would disagree with his concepts, or he would disagree with what I said. Everybody thought we were enemies, but when the meetings were over, we would say, let's have a drink. People would just look at us like, what is going on? We isolated our intellectual disagreements from our friendship, which is the way I think it should be. It is like a marriage. When you are married to somebody you might disagree on a lot of issues, even political issues.

The Chase for Beauty

But it's not the end of your marriage, and it should be the same way with a friend. That is a nice aspect of Dennis's personality."

Dr. Ramirez thought so much of his friend that when his wife wanted a facelift, it was Dr. Hurwitz who he asked to perform the operation. "I knew his work," says Dr. Ramirez, with a note of respect and admiration in his voice. The facelift went well. "Everything was fine. He did a good job, and she had a good result."

Dr. Ramirez learned about Karen's death in time to arrange travel plans to attend the funeral, but he chose not to do so. "It was very difficult for me," he says. It brought back some painful childhood memories.

In the late 1950s, while he was growing up in Peru, his parents had gone on a brief vacation, leaving a babysitter in charge of their four children. During their absence, Dr. Ramirez's older brother, who was 11 years old, went swimming with some friends. "I don't know what happened," says Dr. Ramirez. The only thing he knows for sure is his brother didn't come out of the pool alive. He drowned. His dad was in his late forties at the time. "He lived until he was 84, and, even until the end of his days, he always talked about his son, almost every day. He never forgave himself for having left us with the maid. She was an adult woman who took care of us, but kids are kids. I don't think he ever recovered from that."

About 10 years later, there was more tragedy for the Ramirez family. Dr. Ramirez's teenage sister was on vacation from college and traveling to her aunt's sugarcane farm with some friends. The students never arrived. A car pulled out in front of them on a windy road near the farm. "They were run into a ravine and went into the water," remembers Dr. Ramirez. "They found the bodies of everybody except for my sister. They couldn't find her body. They extricated the car thinking maybe it was stuck in the car. They sent a lot of professional divers to look in different places. They were camping along the river, 30 to 40 people looking for her for a month, going from the place they fell to many miles away, but they couldn't find her."

The search finally came to an end when Dr. Ramirez's father had a dream. His daughter talked to him, says Dr. Ramirez: "'I'm here,' she

The reunited lovebirds in Dennis's yellow GTO convertible. (1965)

The bride and groom with siblings (left to right), Allen Furst, Herbert Furst, Stephen Hurwitz (later adopted his Hebrew name Shimon), Marilyn Hurwitz (later married Dr. Joseph Turner), William Hurwitz. (1969)

Honeymoon summer visiting Paris while living in London and also visiting Edinburgh, Rome, and Stockholm. (1969)

Karen with her father when she was two years old at Cape Cod. (1974)

*Dennis in Jerusalem meeting for the first time with his older brother
after he became an observant Jew. (1975)*

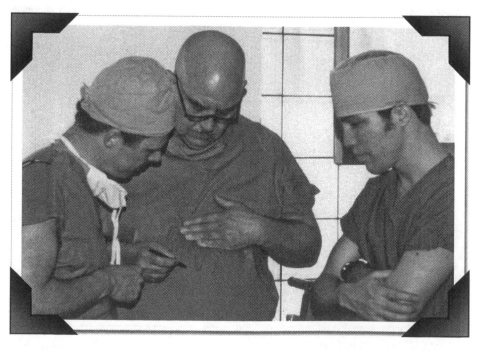

*Chief of Plastic Surgery Dr. Willie L. White instructing Dr. Hurwitz (on right).
(1976)*

Dr. Fernando Ortiz-Monasterio posing with his protégé. (1977)

The Hurwitzes playing in Mellon Park, Pittsburgh. (1978)

Karen reflecting along Cook Forest's Clarion River in photo by her dad during a father-daughter summer canoe trip (just a few months before October 27). (1989)

Karen near her home in Squirrel Hill in a photo by the family's visiting exchange student (just before October 27). This is the Hurwitzes' "Mona Lisa." (1989)

The Hurwitzes leaving the Allegheny County Court house following the murder inquest. (1989)

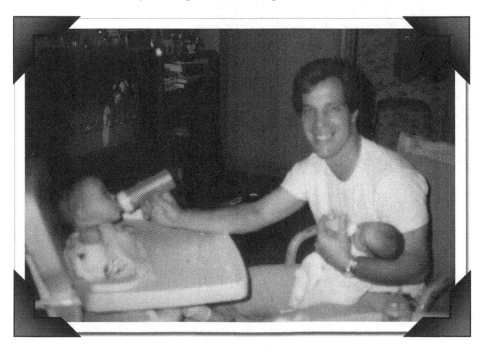

The challenge of having two babies within nine months (which helped renewed their lives). (1990)

The Hurwitzes relaxing inside their Seven Springs resort condo. (1998)

Dr. Hurwitz skiing in the Laurel Mountains near Pittsburgh. (1999)

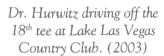

Dr. Hurwitz driving off the 18th tee at Lake Las Vegas Country Club. (2003)

*Dr. Hurwitz posing with Matt Lauer, host of NBC's **Today**,*
after being interviewed on the morning television program. (2005)

The Hurwitzes with their children. (2006)

said, and then she described the area. So, he immediately woke up and told all the workers, 'I know where my daughter is.' They went to look, and she was there."

Once again, he saw the pain his father had to endure: "It was so profound."

When Dr. Ramirez learned of Karen's death, he could only think of his father, and knew he would be of no comfort to his friend. He wondered if Dennis, like his father, would never really recover. "I felt that anything I would say would not alleviate his pain. I didn't go to the funeral."

The pain of Dennis and Linda was evident throughout the service. When Psalm 23 was chanted, Dennis wept uncontrollably. In Rabbi Berkun's eulogy, he talked about sorrow, about loss, about hope, about moving forward. None of the words came easy for the rabbi. "For rabbis," he says, "frankly, you feel you can be of help to people at the time, so you have to get through it. You can't mourn, even though I was mourning. You can't do that. You can't get up there and break down and cry. Then you are of no use."

He completed the eulogy. Everyone was in tears. "It was very tough for me to get through it," he admits, "especially since Karen was someone I knew." He officiated during her Bat Mitzvah just four years earlier. Try as he did, the rabbi's words didn't lessen the pain for Dennis and Linda, or for many others.

"Nobody kept a stiff upper lip. That just wasn't being considered. We all cried," says Marilyn, noting her brother wept especially hard. "I had never seen him so shaken before. He was always the one to think that things will turn out well, I'm going to be successful. This just didn't fit into his game plan at all. He cried a lot."

He never became suicidal, but he could understand how ending one's life can make sense to people faced with incomprehensible misfortune. "Why bother about living, if living is painful, and this is the kind of shit that happens. Why even bother? We're going to die anyhow." Karen's

The Chase for Beauty

murder would eventually provoke suicide attempts by relatives on both sides of the family.

At the time, Dennis didn't share his emotions with his sister. "He was never one to tell you how he feels about something," she says. "This is just another example; he really couldn't talk about it. I don't know what he was thinking."

Not so with Linda. "She was trying so hard to make some sense out of it." Marilyn recalls her consulting with rabbis, looking for answers, hoping for comfort. Marilyn had her own opinion on religion explaining Karen's murder: "Bullshit."

After the funeral, the procession to the cemetery, visible at one point on Pittsburgh's six-lane parkway, seemed to be endlessly long. But the procession did come to an end, as did the burial. The mourning, though, had just begun.

The question was how. Dennis was so angry at God: "He couldn't win on this one, in my mind, as far as getting my respect and admiration. Either He was so impotent that He couldn't stop such terrible things, so who needs Him, or, if this was His design, I certainly didn't like Him. Very simplistic to me. The middle ground was that maybe He could influence this, maybe He couldn't, but I couldn't understand it."

As angry as he was with God, he realized he had to turn to Him. "There is some comfort that with God's help we could get through this without going crazy, or being ineffective individuals, or ruining our lives. We should call upon that spirituality—let formal religion like Judaism take over." Dennis did. "Rather than make up a way to get through this, we pretty closely followed the traditional mourning. It has been around a long time for souls in misery like ours—who wanted to feel better about Karen and get through this—and it must be there for a very good reason."

Shiva is the traditional mourning period in Judaism. Shiva means the number seven in Hebrew; just as it took God seven days to create the world, it takes seven days for a grieving family to return to life. Beginning after the funeral, sitting shiva, what it is most commonly called, often takes place in the home of the deceased for the next seven evenings, excluding the Sabbath. Relatives, friends, and all other mourners go to the home to sit shiva, to pay their respects and recite prayers. The residents of the home are treated like guests, while the actual guests bring the food and serve as hosts. When the seven days pass, the grief isn't meant to end, but it's Judaism's way of saying that it's time to move forward. The individual is not left with the burden of deciding when to mourn and when to return to life's daily responsibilities. Judaism makes that determination for its people, including the Hurwitzes.

"It served its purpose for us," says Dennis. Every night while sitting shiva, the house was full, and many more waited patiently on the street. He and Linda were overwhelmed by the huge response by the community. Karen's classmates came. Old friends like the Wolshes, the Reubens, and the Neimans came. Recent friends came, too, like Jules Rosen, a geriatric psychiatrist and his wife Debbie Fox, a former television reporter. Many members of the Tree of Life Congregation came. So did many people from the medical community and from the Holocaust Center. Even some strangers came.

"We let our misery be somewhat replaced by the good will of people," says Dennis. "They would take their cues. If we wanted to talk about Karen, they would talk about what they remembered about her. If we didn't want to talk about her, they didn't."

To their relief, none of their friends made accusations or were judgmental. In retrospect, it would have been easy to second guess, to ask, "Why was Karen allowed to be friends with someone who had so many problems?" Some strangers weren't so honorable. "We received some anonymous letters," says Linda, "that made some nasty remarks about the black-white relationship and said things like, 'Why was she hanging out with someone like that?'"

Far from holding Karen's parents accountable in any way for what happened, those who knew the Hurwitzes clearly admired how they raised their daughter: "Dennis and Linda invited everybody to their home," says

Harvey Wolsh. "It wasn't a matter of what color you were. I think Karen probably picked up on that when she selected her friends and took them in. You can't blame anybody, there is no blame."

Expressing those same sentiments were Sandy and Louis Kushner. They knew the Hurwitzes through their mutual involvement in Pittsburgh's United Jewish Federation. Their letter of sympathy to Linda and Dennis made poignantly clear that Karen, Linda, and Dennis had done much right, and nothing wrong:

From all that we have heard, you have much to be proud of. Karen's final act was one of the highest mitzvahs and the most noble, helping a friend in trouble. Her actions were an exemplary model of caring and her deeds models for our own children. While it is beyond human comprehension to fathom what resulted, the result should not take away from the noble act that she was performing. It is to your credit as parents that you encouraged her capacity to reach out. It is to Karen's credit that she had the depth of caring and understanding for a friend in trouble.

With much love,

Sandy and Louis Kushner

Many other families tried to do whatever they could to offer comfort to the Hurwitzes during shiva. Two of those families were the Laidholds and the Sussmans, close friends with the Hurwitzes since 1975 when their children and Karen were preschool classmates. Upon learning the news, the Sussmans immediately traveled to Pittsburgh from Louisville, Kentucky, where they had moved in 1980 after Lyle, a college professor, had accepted a position at the University of Louisville. Linda remembers Lyle's wife, Susan, telling her that she just had to stay by her side. Meanwhile, Judy Laidhold, who still lived in Pittsburgh, and two other longtime Hurwitz friends from the community, Priscilla Fadale and Lyn Silverman, came up with an idea. They would create a Karen Hurwitz me-

Chapter Ten

morial fund that would support the kind of activities that Karen embraced as a teenager. The money raised would eventually underwrite *Dragon-breath*, an award-winning literary magazine from Karen's high school. It also enabled the establishment of an endowment that offered financial support to Pittsburgh teenagers who visited Israel and the US Holocaust Memorial Museum in Washington, DC. "Our friends all wanted to do something, anything; everyone felt so devastated," says Linda. "We didn't ask for this. It was spontaneous."

Along with their close friends and the hundreds and hundreds of others who ventured to the Hurwitzes to sit shiva throughout the week, the immediate family was also there, except, of course, Shimon.

Like most children, Dennis, always figured his parents could somehow fix anything. When Steve became Shimon and his parents failed to convince him to return to the United States, Dennis for the first time realized that his parents couldn't change everything. He had that realization again with Karen's death. "My mother was speechless and stupefied by the whole thing, almost catatonic. She was bewildered and hurting, too. So was my father. They were as helpless and dismayed as I was. In a way, they were sensitive enough to back off and not come up with phony solutions or answers or platitudes or how to behave. This wasn't trying to deprogram Shimon."

It also led to a realization for Dennis: "I was on my own."

Linda's parents, Holocaust survivors, had no particular comforting insights to offer, either. The days would be like what Linda's mom first told her: *No one will ever really be able to help you, but you will get through it.*

The lack of parental advice didn't bother Dennis. "All four of them were supportive," he says. "They could have tried to guide us through this, but they saw that the magnitude was too great."

Dennis's brother, Bill, had nothing to say, either. He just listened. It was extremely emotional, obviously," he says. "Dennis commented, as we were doing one of the evening prayers[at shiva], that isn't it amazing how many prayers talk about swords and violence. I keep looking, but I couldn't see it." The brutality of October 27 permeated Dennis's every waking hour, every thought.

There was one visitor who eased Linda's pain. She came the evening after the funeral, once Karen's body was no longer left lingering in the land of the living. Linda had already gone to bed when the visitor came. "I was falling asleep, in that kind of interim kind of phase," she says. The visitor didn't need to ring the doorbell. She went right to the bedroom. The visitor was Karen.

"I felt her come to me and say goodbye," says Linda. "It was like a dream, but she really was there, like a presence, and she kissed me and said, 'I'm dead, but don't worry, I'm okay." She really said goodbye to me. I felt like she was right there with me."

Such an encounter seems more like Hollywood than reality, but Dr. Ramirez's father wouldn't have been skeptical. Neither would authors Bill and Judy Guggenheim. Those two wrote a book called *Hello from Heaven* (New York City: Bantam) that documented more than 350 cases where people were contacted by a deceased family member or friend.

There is another book, *Many Lives, Many Masters* (New York City: Simon and Schuster) by Brian L. Weiss, MD, written in 1988, that had particular meaning for Linda. The book is the case history of one of his patients who was suffering from a variety of psychological problems. The young woman undergoes hypnosis sessions from Dr. Weiss to uncover memories that may be affecting her behavior. What Dr. Weiss finds is that his patient has a history of past lives. The sessions become more profound and personal for Dr. Weiss, a graduate of Columbia University and Yale Medical School, when through his hypnotized patient, he confronts spiritual beings that serve as his patient's guardian in between her past lives. These beings tell Dr. Weiss about his own dead child, along with explaining to him the relevance of his own life. The revelations alleviated the psychological problems of the patient and prompted Dr. Weiss to write about life and immortality.

Chapter Ten

Linda didn't need convincing. "I really did believe that Karen's soul was with me, and it does go on. The book talks about how we travel with the same souls and when we die, it is almost like reincarnation."

Her belief in Karen's immortal soul, her feelings of closure from Karen's goodbye, and her support from her family and friends helped Linda cope with her daughter's murder. But there was something else that helped, too. It was her experience from working at the Holocaust Center. Many of the survivors she interviewed dwelled on why they lived and so many others died. It made her think about death long before Karen's murder. Those thoughts came to the forefront after October 27, 1989.

"I kept thinking that years ago in Europe, before penicillin, everybody lost children. They died, and the parents had to take care of their other children. We, growing up in America, have a fairytale mentality and don't expect children to die. But it happens. It happens! Why should I be surprised bad things happen, knowing what I know? You have to see it as another experience of life, that losing people is part of that whole cycle, and it makes life more precious. It makes you aware of how much you should cherish what you do have and try to make the best of it."

Acceptance, though, is not the same as understanding what happened. "This is still something beyond what I can understand," says Linda, "but I knew I had to keep focusing on life. I think Judaism, as a whole, focuses on life, that you should get through loss and tragedy, and you should still find a way to live."

Dennis was still searching. He, too, read *Many Lives, Many Masters*. "I must admit I was captivated by it," He also read *When Bad Things Happen to Good People* (New York City: Random House) by Rabbi Harold S. Kushner, who was faced with his own child's fatal illness, which prompted him to write the book in 1981. His philosophy resonated with Dennis: "Unlike traditional Judaism, he says this shit just happens. It's not God striking you down."

While the messages of both books gave Dennis some peace, neither eased his malaise. Family and friends couldn't help but notice. "He didn't

The Chase for Beauty

smile," says Marilyn. "Sullen," says Bill. "In shock," says Sandy Neiman. "Dazed," says Jules Rosen. His father must have noticed, too. Dennis didn't have a close relationship with him. None of his children did. "My dad was so tough," says Marilyn. "He had a personality that was not very endearing; he yelled a lot, and he called you names a lot. It just did nothing for your self-esteem when you are treated like that."

By all the children's accounts, he had created a volatile household growing up. He was demanding, argumentative, threatening, unappreciative, and anything but nurturing. He was never a success professionally, and his marriage ended in failure, too. He was a man that Dennis admits having difficulty respecting, and he was just about the last person he would seek out for advice on how to cope with his tragedy. But, it turns out, he didn't have to ask. During the final day of shiva, Mr. Hurwitz made a point to pull his son aside.

"You really ought to consider adoption," he said. Throughout the week of hugs, of hand-holding, of condolences, and many, many tears, no one suggested such a thing. Perhaps it was because of the advancing middle ages of Dennis, 43, and Linda, 41. Perhaps it was because adoption might seem like a way of replacing Karen. Whatever the reason, it wasn't something Dennis and Linda or their thousands of well-wishers ever mentioned.

Dennis didn't take the idea seriously, but for the first time since Karen's death, even if for just a moment, it made him contemplate the future rather than the past. It gave him hope. His father had many shortcomings in the eyes of all his children, but he was the only person in a week of mourning who came up with an approach on how Dennis could move forward in his life.

"In contrast to his usual mercantile, monetary, very limited approach, he was particularly sensitive and I thought almost out of character," says Dennis. "To encourage me to consider adoption was not expected and had all the more impact on me."

Impact, yes, a plan of action, no. The plan of action in Judaism after sitting shiva is to enter the second stage of mourning, called *shloshim*, which means 30 in Hebrew. In the 30 days after the funeral, mourners may return to their routines once shiva is completed, but there should be no entertainment or celebrations—no movies, theater, dances, or parties. For Dennis and Linda, the mourning of Karen would end after shloshim, according to Judaism.

Returning to routines during shloshim meant performing operations for Dennis. Just 10 days after he held his "breathless, beautiful child" in his arms, he went back to work. One of the senior staff doctors was shocked to see him at the hospital. Dennis remembers his colleague's greeting: "You are coming back too soon. You can't do this; you are not yourself."

Dennis didn't listen. "I thought it was enough time." But it didn't feel like enough time. "I remember walking through the hospital hallways like it was going through mud. I just couldn't move. I was so—it was like slow motion. I just didn't have the energy to do anything. I was so drained."

His first operation was scheduled for the next day. It would be on a teenager who had von Recklinghausen disease, which is also known as Elephant man's syndrome. "He was a sadly deformed teenager, around Karen's age," says Dennis. It was up to his doctor to make him look better.

"He had a bilateral cleft lip and palate and also some big lumps on his face—very, very ugly individual—and I had to do so much work to take some of these big things off of his face. It was a very complex operation."

For a while everything went well. "I was sort of getting into it," says Dennis. "It was kind of therapeutic in a way to do what I know how to do. It got my mind off of everything." But there was only so much he or any plastic surgeon could do for the patient. He was too deformed to ever look normal no matter how many medical procedures he underwent. Near the end of the three-hour operation, it dawned on Dennis that he couldn't give his patient a beautiful face.

"I looked at him under anesthesia, and I'm thinking, 'Why is this young man around, and my daughter is not here? This kid will never have a chance in life; living will always be a struggle. What's the sense of all this? My beautiful child is maimed and killed. It makes no sense.'" Dennis's skilled surgeon hands stopped moving. He began to cry while standing over the patient. "I couldn't work anymore," he says. He turned to his senior resident, Dr. Guy Stofman, and asked him to place the final sutures by himself. Then, he walked out. "Operating on this patient, regardless of his appearance, had nothing to do with my daughter," says Dennis, "and yet I couldn't escape it. I couldn't escape it." Dennis had returned to work too soon.

A week later, he tried again, conscientiously making sure he had a qualified senior trainee or surgeon ready to step in, just in case. This time there were no setbacks. He was a plastic surgeon before October 27, 1989, and he would be a plastic surgeon once more. "I could do the work," he says. "What was I going to do? No matter how long I waited, was I going to be any better, or was I going to be more concerned about returning to work?"

Some patients were wary of Dennis's return. Dennis remembers receiving a telephone call from the mother of one his patients, an 8-year-old black child, who was born with a birth defect.

"I guess you don't want to see my son anymore," she says.

"Why?"

"Well, because a young black man killed your daughter. So how could you feel good about seeing my son?"

"I'm sure I am forever changed, but I don't think that is going to be an issue on how I take care of your son, and I am going to have to work through this."

He meant it. "I have my biases and prejudices," he says, "and my comfort level is forever changed. But I don't think the reality has made any difference in my interactions with people."

Chapter Ten

His patient's mother didn't switch doctors, and Dennis rewarded her trust by successfully eliminating the birth defect. Nothing, not even the death of his daughter, could compromise his surgical skills.

Life, though, was another matter for Dennis and Linda. Peace was always fleeting—whether it was the assurance by Linda's mom that they would get through it, or Mick being apprehended and charged with the crime, or Karen's hello to Linda from heaven, or the community's outpouring of sympathy, or the suggestion by Dennis's father to adopt, or finding the "Mona Lisa" picture, or the belief in many lives, many masters. All that any of it provided was a temporary reprieve. Their gaping loss, with seemingly omnipotent power, quickly overpowered any feelings of contentment. Only Karen, as illogical as it was, could make their loss go away.

Dennis found himself looking for her. On his way to work, he would drive through Schenley Park, which borders the campuses of the University of Pittsburgh and Carnegie Mellon University. Coeds, not much older than Karen, would be walking to class. Dennis would think the unthinkable, that one of them might turn around and be his daughter. He knew it wasn't rational, but his mind wouldn't allow him to believe that the beautiful face he knew so well would never be seen again. "It was reality that was unreal," he says. Day after day during shloshim, he'd pull into his office parking lot, without having caught a glimpse of his child. Tomorrow, the day after tomorrow, the week after tomorrow, the lifetime after tomorrow would all be the same. There would be a fruitless search for Karen. For the first time in Dennis's life, his future was stagnant; instead of moving forward, he was anchored in the past. It's a weight so strong that some men, like Dr. Ramirez's father, can never break free. Life becomes past tense.

"I was just going through the motions," says Dennis. "Doing surgery, coming home, having meals, I won't say aimlessly, but with no real sense of where we were heading." Should he and Linda move from the house? Should they leave Pittsburgh? Should they leave each other?

The Chase for Beauty

It's never a surprise when the happiest, strongest marriages dissolve in the wake of tragedy. Would each of them be a constant reminder to each other of what they had lost? Would they blame each other for what happened? Would their grief overpower everything, including their love for each other? They didn't know.

The first test came at the end of shiva. It was permissible to make love again in the eyes of God. They reached out and found the familiar comfort of each other's touch. Their intimacy hadn't been destroyed. "What happened was not about us," says Dennis, "it is about Karen." Together, not separated, seemed right—at night and during the day.

They were never far away from each other. Both of their offices and the hospital where Dennis operated were in Oakland. Throughout shloshim, they called each other regularly while at work. "We'd keep asking, 'How are you doing?' 'Are you doing okay?' 'Do you need to meet for a cup of coffee or something?'" says Linda. "I think we were both trying to be really responsive and sensitive to each other."

They shunned professional help. "We were told about many support groups, parents of violently killed children. We had no interest," says Dennis. "We weren't happy, but we were able to work, we were able to eat, and we didn't think that these people had any more insights than we already had."

Their friends weren't so sure that was a good idea. Mara, Roz, Debbie, and some others had a talk with Linda. "We sat Linda down," remembers Roz, "and said we really think that you and Dennis need to see somebody, you need a professional. She looked at us and said, 'That's ridiculous; I've got you guys.'"

The friends' "cocoon" protecting the Hurwitzes continued throughout shloshim. They made a schedule so someone was always at the Hurwitzes to make dinner, watch television with them, talk with them, cry with them. They were rarely alone.

Dennis had his work, had his wife, had his friends, but he didn't have his daughter. And that thought wouldn't go away. "I was going more in a shell and felt alone," he says. "I found ways to blame myself for what happened. We think we are so controlling that we can make things happen, things not happen."

It got to the point that the love of his life, the only one who could understand his misery, couldn't help. "I was not getting strength from Linda. Maybe it was there for me to absorb, but maybe it wasn't. She was dealing with her own sense of guilt. I didn't see her as a source of strength. I was looking around for a source of strength; I thought she was just as troubled. She kept intermittently dwelling on the fact that she didn't get up with Karen that night."

Dennis did what he could to ease her pain. He talked it out logically. What if she had gone downstairs with Karen on October 27? How does she know she could have saved Karen? How does she know he wouldn't have killed her, too? How did she know that Mick wouldn't have done what he did on another night? Those were his words of absolution, but they weren't words he necessarily believed.

"I was fighting not being angry with her myself," he says. "I didn't say this to her, but I would have hoped that she would have gone downstairs with Karen. Because not going down didn't save her, so going down might have."

He knew better than to place blame. "Getting angry with Linda of what she may or may have not done does not save Karen and does not help our marriage. It is not a good thing to think that way, and what lesson is there, really? It would be easy for me to blame her and take some of the pressure off of me, but once that starts, it will cascade into you should have done this and you should have done that. We can't undo what happened anyhow."

Dennis wanted to move forward, but he didn't know how. The world had no beauty anymore. Only questions. He and Linda continued to contemplate the answers.

Many of Pittsburgh's rabbis had offered answers. One rabbi said to Dennis just after the funeral that what happened was predetermined. People can choose what newspaper they read or what they will eat for dinner. But the book of life was solely in God's hands.

Another answer came from a rabbi who was orthodox, the most religious of the Jewish movements. He spoke to the Hurwitzes during the last night of sitting shiva. "He told a story about souls," says Linda, "that Jews really believe souls travel together and that we should just think of Karen's soul as having gone on the journey ahead of us, but we will catch up with her eventually."

"So," adds Dennis, "if you are going to always see somebody ultimately, why are you so upset when they die? The metaphor was, it is like a ship that is going on a tremendous voyage, and we will have to catch up with Karen later. That is comforting. Tragedies are not so devastating when you consider the eternity of existence. It is a buffer. But it doesn't get rid of the sadness."

Perhaps the best answer, though, came from another orthodox rabbi from the Lubavitch community. He happened to be in Pittsburgh attending a Lubavitch retreat. Some of the members of the Pittsburgh Lubavitch community knew the Hurwitzes and told the visiting rabbi what happened.

"Friends called and asked if the rabbi could come over," says Linda. "He wanted to meet us and see if he could be of any comfort." Linda had no objections. Shloshim was nearing its end, but Dennis and Linda were still in deep mourning. Not long after the rabbi arrived, he gazed at the newly framed picture hanging in the den. It was Linda's Mona Lisa. When he was done scrutinizing the picture, Linda remembers him turning to her and Dennis and saying, "She had a 17-year-old soul." The concept resonated with Linda in particular. The rabbi had more to say. "A life is a life, whether it is seven hours, seven days, 17 years, or 70 years. It should be cherished for whatever it is. We don't know when we are born how long we will live. It could be seven hours and, if it is, it is still a cherished soul."

What he said next really surprised Linda.

Chapter Ten

121

"Your daughter had a very fragile *neshama*, a very fragile soul. Maybe that's why you didn't have more kids. She needed both of you. Maybe now things will change and you will have more children."

"It was very spiritual," says Linda, "because Dennis and I had already started to talk about that, but we hadn't said anything to anybody yet."

Dennis knew they had to do something, had to start moving forward again. It became very apparent to him during Thanksgiving at Marilyn and Joe's home just a few days before the Lubavitch rabbi's visit. The three Turner children and a half-dozen guests were there along with Dennis and Linda. Even the Turner's seven-year-old-son, Michael, perceived the holiday's emptiness. Marilyn told Linda that her toddler said, "Uncle Dennis and Aunt Linda are still sad." The dinner conversation was practically nonexistent. Karen must have been in everyone's thoughts

Finally, Dennis broke the silence. "I'm determined that something good will come of all this," he declared. He just wasn't sure what it would be. He and Linda talked later that evening about calling Magee-Womens Hospital and trying the in vitro pregnancy procedure once again.

When the Lubavitch rabbi talked about more children it made Linda think again of the gypsy at the Hungarian restaurant. The catastrophic event in her early forties had certainly happened. Would Linda now have twins as the gypsy predicted?

"From then on," Linda says of the rabbi's visit, "I had it in my head that if I went through in vitro again, I was going to get pregnant with twins."

She called Magee. "They weren't surprised to hear from us," says Linda. It turned out the procedure is not one that the hospital offers to women more than 40 years old. Linda's doctor didn't care. "They broke the rules," says Dennis. It was as if everyone in the community wanted to lessen the Hurwitzes' pain.

Dennis found himself thinking more and more about who experienced the most pain. "I guess everyone who loses someone, it's almost a selfish thing—look what she did to me, she died on me. I shouldn't feel bad for

The Chase for Beauty

feeling bad for my loss, but you have to almost purposely realize what it's about is that's she's not here to enjoy her own life, fulfill her own blessing. And, maybe, to a lesser degree, for a wonderful person like Karen, the world is missing a little bit that she's not here. The world can't afford to lose a lot of people like that. Everybody loses—we lost, the world lost. And, of course, she is the biggest loser. She was robbed of her life."

If she was robbed, then someone must be guilty of stealing. Mick's punishment was up to the legal system. Shimon intimated, though, that Karen's death might have been a message from God. The Lubavitch rabbi reinforced Dennis's thoughts about placing blame. "Don't waste your energy blaming yourselves or anyone else, because it's futile," he said to Dennis and Linda. "There is not an answer for this kind of thing as to why it happened. The question is how are you going to live your life in light of the fact that it happened."

Living their life wasn't easy. Reminders of their loss were everywhere. "People kept calling me Karen, because when they saw me that is what they were thinking about," says Linda. "I felt very conspicuous."

It was no different at home. On Karen's bedroom desk was her college application to Boston University. "It was ready to go," says Linda. That lost future was accentuated when the Hurwitzes received a letter, addressed to Karen, dated November 15, 1989. It was from Boston University's director of admissions, Frederic A. Siegel. He wrote:

We hope that you will continue to explore Boston University's nine undergraduate colleges by actually applying. If there is any help you need during the application process, please feel free to call me.

"I never had the heart to respond," says Linda.

Dennis and Linda gave thought to everything the rabbis said. They began the in vitro procedure. Dennis even began considering adoption. None of it ended their mourning, though, even though shloshim had been completed. Both of them desperately wanted to move forward, and they were making attempts do just that, but there were still so many unanswerable questions. Nothing about their future was guaranteed. Nothing.

Chapter Ten

"Somebody suggested that maybe we should go away by ourselves for a couple of days," says Linda. Get away from the ongoing newspaper headlines, the stares from strangers, the house and city where their daughter's life ended. The idea made sense to Dennis and Linda. They left Pittsburgh. Would they ever return?

Chapter Eleven

Tranquility. Merriment. Beauty. Paradise. All were missing from the lives of Dennis and Linda since October 27. But all were advertised to exist on a tiny island along Florida's Gulf Coast. The grieving couple didn't know what to expect when they arrived in Captiva. They wanted to forget, but they wanted to remember. They wanted to laugh, but they wanted to cry. They wanted to move forward, but they wanted to go backward. They wanted direction. They needed direction.

Choices for tourists throughout the island are many—walking the pristine, white-sand beaches famous for their exotic seashells and beautiful sunsets; bike riding along the paths that zigzag across the island; browsing through the many art galleries and studios of artists who capture the island's laid-back charm; windsurfing for the adventurous; bird watching for those who want to keep their feet on the ground; deep-sea fishing for the Papa Hemingway sect; or just curling up with a good book in the land where Spanish explorer Juan Ponce de Leon once searched for the Fountain of Youth.

The choices become more limited when the weather doesn't cooperate. Dennis and Linda found that out when the sun that is featured so prominently in vacation brochures seemed hesitant to make an appearance. The bad weather gave them more time to think about each other, about having more children, about Pittsburgh, and, of course, about Karen.

Linda didn't need more time to think about her marriage. She realized losing Karen didn't end her love for her husband. "If something like this had happened when we were in Dartmouth, and I was feeling very detached, I probably would have split," she admits. "But by the time Karen was murdered, we were back in sync, both feeling very connected to each other. We had fallen back in love again."

Dennis wasn't wavering, either. "I think about life in regard to what is desirable. When it came to choosing my life's avocation, I picked medicine, not so much for all the great things in it, and there are, but because I didn't see anything else I really liked doing. Nothing was good enough in comparison to medicine. I feel the same way about Linda. Nobody compares to her. So, I don't really think of her as an angel sent from heaven; it is just that everybody else falls short. She has things about her that I wish were a little different, but the package is pretty darn good—more than pretty darn good, it is phenomenal, and in no moment in time have I ever coveted another person to live my life with. I won't say there hasn't been some sexual attraction from other women over the years, but not to be my mate. In the context of the tragedy, I know friends told us, and I knew myself, that our marriage was in jeopardy and being tested, but I didn't want to test it. So, I avoided a few issues that could really send us in a tailspin."

Linda and Dennis were staying together *for better, or worse* as long as they both shall live. In an unspoken way, Captiva renewed those vows. But for Dennis, the getaway highlighted the emptiness in his life. "We stayed at a very nice resort, very pleasant. But I had this sense that if we had no children that much of our life would be doing stuff like this, and that really wasn't all that fulfilling, going to nice resorts and going to beaches. It is not really what I like. I like hard work and doing surgery and raising kids."

The in vitro procedure gave Dennis and Linda some hope that they could have more children. They both realized, though, that pregnancy was far from a sure thing. Linda had undergone the procedure nearly a half-dozen times with no luck in the past few years. Now, she was more than 40 years old, which so significantly reduced her chances for a successful pregnancy that hospital age requirement rules had to be ignored for her involvement in the program.

They even inquired about Marilyn serving as a surrogate mother if that could enhance the chances of a baby's birth. "She had offered to carry for us," says Dennis. Unfortunately, that, too, was against hospital rules. Top-level administrators conducted a hearing to consider the Hurwitzes' request. "They wouldn't let her do it," says Dennis.

The advice he received from his father at the end of sitting shiva started to have more and more clarity and relevance. Since Karen's murder, he couldn't bare the thought of not having a child, of his child not having a child, of his grandchild not having a child. Children, to Dennis, were the reason to exist. They were immortality. Without them, life, with all its personal drama, was fleeting—merely taking a tiny speck of time from all eternity. He just had to hear someone call him "Dad" again.

He made up his mind that he and Linda should adopt. "Let me say," he reveals, "I wasn't exactly sure it was the right route. It's the same aphorism of surgery: *I may not be right, but I'm sure.*

"Listen, people make decisions in life whether buying a car or a house. They decide—'I don't know if this is right, but I'm going to do it.' That happens all the time, making decisions on less-than-ideal information. That is the nature of surgery." It was also the nature of Dennis's adoption logic.

He had to convince Linda, and she needed convincing. The two of them had many friends, many adult interests, successful dual careers. If the in vitro procedure wasn't successful, Linda could envision a future without children. "I think," she says, "when you talk about certain marriages, the marriage is stronger or being a parent is stronger. I think, for us, our marriage is number one and being a parent is number two."

Captiva served as a backdrop for a debate in which neither one knew who was right. Dennis, with his surgeon's mentality, pressed hard. "My job, as I saw it, was to prepare for the future and to see that Linda saw it my way—that we start up a family again and try the adoption process."

The conversation went wherever they traveled on the island, even on a boat cruise. While they stood together on the deck overlooking the water,

Linda began to acquiesce. "I sort of accepted it," she says, "because part of me was afraid I'd lose him if I didn't. I thought, 'If it's that important for him, I have to do it for him.'"

As Dennis glanced toward the sky and Linda peered at the water, they both contemplated privately whether adoption truly made sense. They both saw the answer.

"I literally saw Karen's image in the cloud formation," says Dennis.

"I saw this image of Karen reflected in the way the light was on the water," says Linda.

"I saw her in a very relaxed mode, her face," adds Dennis. The image in the sky reminded him of the father-and-daughter drive the two of them took about a year earlier. They were going to visit one of Dennis's cleft palate patients—a 12-year-old boy. "He was severely deformed, no nose," says Dennis. To make matters worse, his parents had died from cancer. Doctors, particularly surgeons, aren't supposed to become too emotionally attached to their patients, but Dennis couldn't help himself from feeling sorry for the youngster. There was only so much he could do surgically. Yet, he wanted to do more. That's when adoption came to mind.

He worried, though, that Karen might feel jealous or threatened. She didn't. When Dennis asked her what she thought, he remembers her thinking it over and then saying, "I think it is a good thing, and I will be all right."

She even kept her dad company on that drive to get the young boy and bring him to the Hurwitz home for a visit.

Ultimately, the adoption never happened. "He was already 12. He was raised as a Christian and raised out in the country. We were Jewish, living in the city; culturally it would be so different. It would have been too much for him," explains Linda. "Karen was willing. She was responsive. It was me who couldn't do it. I told Dennis I couldn't do it."

"The point was Karen was sympathetic and supportive," says Dennis.

"She had a beautiful heart," adds Linda. "She was such a good person."

On that boat off the shore of Captiva, Dennis and Linda saw their own image of Karen. For each of them, it was only her face, but both felt her beautiful heart.

"I believed at that moment that she was accepting of us moving forward with more children," says Dennis.

Linda agrees: "It was her spirit following us, giving us guidance. It was an amazing spiritual moment."

Linda didn't need further convincing. She and Dennis made plans before the boat ride ended. Michale Anderson had taken away their daughter. But he wouldn't take away their love for each other. He wouldn't take away their city. And he wouldn't take away their family; provided, that is, they were given one.

Chapter Twelve

The few days spent in Captiva gave Dennis a goal that could possibly spare him the kind of future that persecuted Dr. Ramirez's father. He and Linda still grieved for Karen. Every day the parents without a child shed tears. Neither could envision a time when they wouldn't cry or question God or feel sorry for themselves. But when they returned to their home in Pittsburgh, Dennis had a reason to get out of bed other than to mundanely go through the motions of life. With Linda's blessing, Karen's too, he would try to start a family for the second time.

He certainly wasn't going to depend on the in vitro procedure being successful. Instead, he began to follow, in earnest, his father's suggestion. The quest didn't get off to the best of starts. "It was not very reassuring early on," says Dennis. "We were told we were too old for public adoption."

Undaunted, he turned to the private adoption process. Somewhere, there was a pregnant woman carrying the Hurwitzes' child. It was up to Dennis to find that stranger. He and Linda met with a social worker who gave them suggestions on where and how to look. The search had to be very public. The baby could come through the networking of friends and acquaintances, or through an advertisement in a college newspaper, or even through a flyer posted in a coin laundry. The broad approach made sense to Dennis. He and Linda did it all, even the flyers in coin laundries. "I went around and tacked them up there," he says.

Linda couldn't muster the same kind of enthusiasm for the search, but she wasn't surprised by her husband's drive. "It was so typical of Dennis," she says, "directing energy toward something positive."

"It was a goal, something to work for," shrugs Dennis. "The Thomas Edison approach: try a lot of things, something will work."

He had no misgivings, not after Captiva, and not after a Hanukkah dinner at the home of Linda's brother, Herb, who lived with his wife and two children in Rockville, Maryland. Also there for the holiday celebration was Linda's other brother, Allen, and his wife and two children. The holiday commemorates the Jewish people reclaiming Jerusalem's Temple from their Syrian oppressors around 165 BCE. When the victors went to light the *ner tamid*, the eternal light of the Temple, they could find only enough holy oil to last one evening. Miraculously, though, the light stayed lit for eight days, until more holy oil was available. From the standpoint of most Jewish children, Hanukkah, the Festival of Lights, is the Jewish version of Christmas, because they get a present each of the holiday's eight nights.

The children eagerly opened one of their presents that first night. Dennis and Linda watched in great pain. "It was dreadful," says Dennis. "How was I going to have one special occasion after another and have no children? Life felt hollow and incomplete."

Rather than the Hanukkah experience immobilizing him in sadness, it gives him even more energy for his Thomas Edison approach. Not everyone was so enthusiastic. For the first time, there were a few cracks in their "cocoon" of friends and family. "It's too soon," many of them suggested. Surprisingly, one of their critics was Marilyn, even though she had offered to be a surrogate mother for them.

"Part of me was thinking it's not like your dog died, and you could buy a new dog," she says, "I was a little nervous about them trying to replace Karen so soon." In Dennis's mind, though, he was not replacing his daughter. Karen was 17 years old, not an infant. Besides, there was no time to wait. He was 43 years old and Linda was just two years younger. Most people that age are about to become grandparents, not parents.

The adoption criticism from those who were close to Dennis and Linda bewildered and angered Roz's husband, Sandy. "People never cease to amaze me, and this was one of the more amazing things, that others had the audacity to be judgmental about Dennis and Linda's decision making, and to tell them so—that these friends even have a thought as to what Dennis and Linda should do in the face of such tragedy."

His wife, Roz, tried to combat the questioning comments Linda was hearing. "I sat her down and said, 'Your house is too empty. You have to fill this house' and she said, 'I know I do.'" Dennis didn't need a pep talk. "He was adamant to do it," says Roz. "Linda was reticent, but Linda is reticent to do anything. Linda has the brakes in the relationship."

Like the Neimans, the Rosens completely supported the Hurwitzes' wishes. Jules Rosen, a geriatric psychiatrist, refrained from giving any unsolicited recommendations.

"They never asked me for advice, and I learned a long time ago that gratuitous psychiatric advice is not only unwelcome, but it is usually wrong. How did anyone really know what they were going through? If they had asked me for advice, I would have then explored with them where they were in the grief process. Theoretically, were they shoving their grief under the rug and replacing it with a child? I might have asked them questions about how they thought about this."

As a friend, he never felt the need to voice his opinion. "I never had second thoughts of them adopting. I think they knew what they needed to do. Clearly, bringing a baby into their life wouldn't diminish their capacity of grief for Karen. It wouldn't be a replacement of Karen. It would be the growth of a family."

And that's what the Hurwitzes wanted, what Dennis needed. Just after Karen's murder, Dr. Rosen remembers Dennis saying to him, "I didn't waste 17 years of my life raising a child, and I don't want to be without children. I see myself with kids."

Marilyn, while not in total agreement with the decision, admired their courage. "I felt if I had lost my only child, I could have never started all over again. That is just the way I am." She was not alone in that feeling. But in Dennis's mind, there was no debate. Having a child would be his future, the only future he would accept.

Chapter Twelve

His willed future came—not from the flyers and not from the newspaper advertisements. It came from their circle of friends. The friend of a friend happened to be married to an obstetric gynecologist. That doctor had a pregnant patient who was beginning her third trimester, but she didn't want to keep the baby. After a flurry of phone calls, and some work by attorneys, it was decided the Hurwitzes would be a mom and dad again. They wouldn't be getting twins, like the gypsy predicted, but Linda wasn't complaining.

Just slightly more than a month after Captiva, Jeffrey Samuel Hurwitz was delivered by Caesarean section. He was nearly two months premature and weighed only 3 pounds 5 ounces. His birth mother had become toxic, which prompted the early birth. Both were fine. So were Jeffrey's new parents.

"He was so precious from the moment we saw him," says Linda. Until he gained some weight, he had to stay in the hospital, so Dennis and Linda became regulars in the newborn intensive care unit. "We fell in love with him immediately."

All parents know that new love doesn't diminish old love. Linda and Dennis still loved and missed Karen. "I would cry in the shower, cry in my car," says Linda. On his way to work, Dennis still looked for Karen's smile somewhere among the college students in the park. He and Linda were trying their best, but their days still had many random moments of pain.

On January 25, Jeffrey, who weighed 4 pounds 7 ounces, was waiting for Mom to pick him up and take him home. When Linda arrived, she brought along a urine sample for testing, just in case the in vitro procedure had performed a second miracle. Not long after Jeffrey settled into his new neighborhood. The telephone rang. The call came from the hospital. Or was it the gypsy? Linda was pregnant. When she hung up the telephone, she thought of the gypsy. She also thought of her husband.

"When he said something good would come out of Karen's death at Thanksgiving, and here we get Jeffrey within a month and a half, and then I find out that same day that I'm pregnant, it had truly happened. We were

The Chase for Beauty

going to be parents of two kids. It felt so good to be excited about something. There was this newness of a whole new start, and we were thrilled. It didn't matter how they were coming."

Dennis had done it. His friend Sandy was in awe at the courageousness of both of them. "Given what they had gone through, were still going through, it was an amazing affirmation of life."

For the most part, their friends' division on whether to adopt vanished as soon as Jeffrey was born. Everyone wanted to meet the newest Hurwitz. No one knew about his *twin*. "I remember people coming over, and I'm not telling anyone what I'm going through, and I remember sitting on our recliner with my legs up, not doing anything," says Linda. "I didn't offer anybody something to drink or eat. Nothing. I just wanted to hold on to this baby, give it the best shot possible." She was thinking like a mother again.

Dennis had no trouble thinking like a father again. His problem was thinking like a plastic surgeon again. He had resumed standard office hours and performed operations regularly; to his patients and colleagues and even some of his office staff, it appeared that he had recovered, at least professionally, from Karen's death. But, he hadn't. His world of beauty that fueled his surgical art had changed on October 27. Since then, the chase for beauty didn't seem to have the same relevance anymore. One person who noticed was his office manager, Kathy Ottaviano. "I remember a lot of times walking back to his office, he was just kind of zoned," says Kathy, "staring out the window, that kind of thing. I could tell he was ready to go home at night, too; he wasn't going to stay in the office late like he used to."

The career of another plastic surgeon, Scott Spear, hadn't been sidetracked. He was a professor at Georgetown University and was second in command of the university hospital's plastic surgery department. Like most renowned plastic surgeons, his search for beauty wasn't confined to the operating room or the doctor's office. It was a part of his life on weekends, vacations, anytime. A dozen or so plastic surgeons in Western

Chapter Twelve

Europe had the same life, and they came up with an ingenious idea—combine a vacation with their passion. They formed the Alpine Workshop in Plastic Surgery in the early 1970s. Every winter, the workshop's doctors and a few invited colleagues would meet at the top of the Alps or some other majestic snow-covered mountain range. They would spend the week furthering the profession by discussing their latest techniques while they were on the slopes, in the conferences rooms, or at dinner.

Dr. Spear had been an invited colleague to a couple of the workshops and was impressed, especially in comparison to national society meetings, which usually have thousands of members in attendance. "You go to those meetings and walk by people, and you don't know any of them," says Dr. Spear. He noted that an impersonal atmosphere didn't exist at the workshop. "With 20 or 30 people, you usually know them all; it's a much nicer feeling." These friendships could also make the national meetings, with 30 recognizable faces, a bit less shrouded in anonymity.

Dr. Spear was so impressed with this kind of camaraderie that in the spring of 1989 he and a few of his esteemed American colleagues decided to establish the American Alpine Workshop in Plastic Surgery. "We have mountains and snow and accomplished surgeons," he says. "We could do the same thing." Their first workshop would be held in Snowmass, Colorado, in early February 1990.

Just like their European counterparts, the founders wanted the workshop to be much more than a ski trip. There would be three-hour meetings every day starting around dusk, and then there would be a group dinner where medical discussions could continue. Only elite plastic surgeons would be considered. "It was reserved for people who are considered not just plastic surgeons, but particularly good plastic surgeons—contributors, academic types," says Dr. Spear. "We set the bar pretty high." Invitations wouldn't be extended to anyone who wasn't a member of the American Association of Plastic Surgeons, which was founded in 1921 with a mission to *advance the science and art of plastic surgery through surgical education, research, scientific presentations, and professional*

interaction. Membership in that association is by invitation only: *candidates must show recognized contributions of quality in the field of plastic surgery as a prerequisite to membership. They will be expected to have made outstanding contributions to the field of plastic surgery in the areas of education, research, or clinical excellence.*

Dennis met all the criteria for the workshop. He became a member of the AAPS in 1987 and belonged to 16 other professional medical organizations. He was frequently consulted by other physicians, especially on general flap reconstruction and cleft lip and palate repair. Also, he had originated and popularized the gluteal thigh flap procedure—often referred to as the Hurwitz flap—which is performed during reconstructive surgery around the buttocks. He lectured throughout the nation and around the world, on a wide range of plastic surgery subjects. He taught both medical students and peers in plastic surgery, and he had published 27 peer reviewed articles and 22 book chapters for scientific publications on subjects such as facelift, reconstructive surgery, and vascular malformations. While at Dartmouth, he also found time to become an excellent skier.

Dr. Spear had met Dennis at a few meetings and case consults. "I didn't know him all that well, but I knew him a little bit," says Dr. Spear. "Plastic surgeons are familiar with other plastic surgeons in sort of a vague way, either by having read something they wrote or having listened to them in a presentation type thing."

Eventually, the news of Karen's murder reached plastic surgeons throughout the country, including Dr. Spear. Unforeseen death had recently touched his life. His sister's teenage daughter died in an automobile accident. During his mourning, he had an idea. "It struck me that it would be a very nice thing to invite Dennis to the workshop. It's a gift to have the opportunity to do the right thing. It is like you see somebody stranded on the side of the road in the pouring rain, and what a great gift it is to stop the car and rescue them."

His decision to offer Dennis an invitation didn't meet any resistance from the workshop's founding group. They knew he was qualified to be a part of the group.

Chapter Twelve

Dr. Spear called Dennis in late January with the invitation. The offer was unexpected. "He had to stop and think about it, collect himself, and discuss it with Linda," says Dr. Spear. He didn't realize that Dennis had just become the father of a baby boy.

Aside from that news, it struck Dr. Spear that his invitee still seemed to be in a "state of shock" over what happened. He didn't know what Dennis would do. Neither did Dennis. After talking it over with Linda, who was supportive of the trip, he told Dr. Spear he would accept the invitation.

The trip was just a few weeks away, and the resort had no more room vacancies, so Dr. Spear and Dennis would be roommates for the week. The uneasiness over Dennis's recent history didn't bother Dr. Spear. For surgeons, there is no hiding from death.

The two accomplished plastic surgeons got to know each other very well, says Dr. Spear. "We pretty much skied together every day, riding the chairlift a lot— so we were talking on the chairlift and, of course, we were talking in the room at night." The conversation wasn't typical man-to-man conversation. "We spent a lot of time talking about things, basically about life, death, and dying. Dennis was in the middle of trying to sort out his feelings."

He talked with Dr. Spear about the books he had read, about the conversations with rabbis, about Karen. The conversations went deep into the night. "I think I was just mostly listening," says Dr. Spear. "It really was sort of a grief counseling session that went on for a week in the mountains. I think he was questioning whether he had a right to go on with his life as before or whether he should sort of, in a sense, be in mourning. One of the reasons why I wanted him to come was the idea that life goes on. Essentially, what I was doing was giving him the opportunity to start his life up. I think what he was doing was trying to decide if this was the right moment. I think what happened was—as his decision to come to Colorado reflected—that he had decided he was ready, ready to get back into it."

The assessment by Dr. Spear seemed accurate. Dennis always lived his life full speed ahead. The past few months he basically shut his engine off for the first time in his life. He was ready to rev up again. "The workshop was very therapeutic," says Dennis. The conversations and the ski slopes brought back his chase for beauty.

"I'm not a great skier, but I swoop slopes pretty well. I ski must faster and harder than most people my age."

Dr. Spear concurs. "He is a much better skier than I am."

"It helps me stay fit and mentally alert," explains Dennis. "I have a lot of skiing metaphors when I teach surgery. Skiing really sets you up for this instant danger that can be mostly avoided by awareness and good form and fitness. It forces you to concentrate, and it's a great feeling. I prepare myself for surgery like I prepare myself to go down a difficult ski slope—with intensity and alertness and with a sense of expectation, of looking forward to it. You don't ski difficult slopes because you dread them; you ski them because you look forward to the challenge and the circumstances, the environment, the feel, and the air. I'm one to soak in experience and not let it get past me, because it will come and go and I want to be aware what is going on around me, so that I can respond appropriately."

He was ready to resume the chase again.

When he returned to Pittsburgh, though, there was more sadness to confront. Linda lost the *twin* that nobody knew about. She and her husband did what had become so natural. They cried together. "I was sad for my loss," says Dennis, "but I was most sad for Linda's loss. I hurt for my wife. It was another mourning now."

Linda told Dennis there would be no more in vitro procedures. "I can't go through this again. No more losses," she told him. Dennis didn't argue. They had Jeffrey, and they hadn't given up on adopting more children.

Sure enough, their network of friends came through again. They led the Hurwitzes to another pregnant woman who didn't want to keep her child. Perhaps Jeffrey would have a *twin* after all. Although, before long, Dennis wasn't so sure. The birth mother seemed to be very demanding as she continually asked for help paying more and more of her living expenses. When she asked the Hurwitzes to pay her mortgage, Dennis had enough of her demands. He knew there was no guarantee she wouldn't renege once the baby was born. In a court of law, birth mothers always have the right to keep their babies. There is no such thing as an ironclad agreement. As much as Dennis and Linda wanted Jeffrey to have a brother or sister, this didn't seem to be the one. They would wait and hope for another soul to come their way.

In the meantime, Jeffrey was finally ready for his bris, which is a brief religious ceremony and circumcision for Jewish newborn males. Bris means covenant in Hebrew, and the circumcision is a sign of the covenant between God and the baby. The circumcision is performed by a mohel—someone who is Jewish, trained in the procedure, and understands the religious significance of the ritual. Typically, the bris takes place in the home when the baby is eight days old, but it was delayed until mid March in Jeffrey's case, because he was born prematurely. The cutting is quick and relatively painless, judging by babies rarely crying for more than a few moments afterward. If there are any medical concerns, they are usually for one of the guests who isn't used to seeing someone cut. Most mohels are used to dealing with a light-headed adult once the ceremony is over.

Sure enough, there was one adult who had difficulties at Jeffrey's bris. It was someone no one would have expected. "Dennis was such a wreck," says Linda. "I've never seen him sweat like that."

Dennis had a simple, yet telling, explanation. "It was another knife to a child of mine. That may be bizarre, but I was just uncomfortable with the bris, cutting off Jeffrey's flesh."

Grim reminders of Karen's fate were still everywhere, even at the happiest of occasions. When there weren't the obvious reminders, the specter of the upcoming Michale Anderson trial loomed in the minds of Dennis and Linda. And, of course, every time the Hurwitzes went home, they revisited the crime scene.

While those who knew the Hurwitzes debated, sometimes angrily, whether the couple should adopt, no one would question them for selling

The Chase for Beauty

the house. It was expected. Roz, a real estate agent, showed them a few homes that were for sale in the neighborhood. But after the tours, Dennis and Linda always made the same choice—neither wanted to move from their dream home. It was the same resolve that surfaced at Captiva. Michale Anderson would not take away their house and the loving memories it held.

"I look at the backyard and I see Karen throwing a Frisbee," says Dennis. "She could throw it very well, frankly. She couldn't throw a baseball or catch a baseball; it would hit her in the face. But she could play Frisbee. We did it so much. I see her there. But it's not painful. It's kind of wistful. She's never really far from us."

The Hurwitzes weren't moving.

The Chase for Beauty

Chapter Thirteen

Nearly eight months after the nightmare of October 27, 1989, it was far from over. Michale Anderson's trial for the criminal homicide of Karen Hurwitz began on June 18, 1990.

The defense and the prosecution were in agreement that Mick killed Karen. The question to be answered by a jury concerned Mick's state of mind on October 27. If the jury believed he had diminished mental capacity, the court would have to rule that he didn't kill Karen in an intentional, deliberate, and premeditated manner. Such a finding would be a tremendous victory for the defense, because it would preclude a first-degree murder conviction and a sentence of life behind bars with no parole. Instead, he would be convicted of either third-degree murder or voluntary manslaughter. For third-degree murder, the defendant would face from 10 to 20 years in prison, and for voluntary manslaughter, he would be imprisoned for five to 10 years. To Dennis and Linda, the thought of Mick ever being free again would be a blunder of *Clockwork Orange* proportions. "The world would be even less safe than it already is," says Dennis.

In preparing Mick's defense, Jon Botula, a court-appointed attorney, asked the court on June 5 for more time to explore psychiatric information, especially regarding his client's hospital confinement after his suicide attempt in the summer of 1988:

I am requesting a continuance in this matter in order that I'm able to develop a sufficient psychological and psychiatric profile on this man because the Commonwealth is prosecuting a first-degree murder case; my only defense at this point is that of diminished capacity. And it's my position that it will not be properly prepared on or before June 18.

The request was denied, but Mr. Botula did secure from the court the release of a behavioral clinic social service report. That included postmurder psychiatric evaluations of Mick. Three years later, in testimony under oath during an evidentiary hearing, Mr. Botula explained his game plan for the trial:

"After analyzing these reports that were given to me, comparing the content with what had previously been told to me by a psychologist that examined Mr. Anderson, and my own observations and impressions, I did nothing further in respect to pursuing a professional examination of Mr. Anderson.... I felt that based on his confession, the manner in which the confession was elicited, and in his discussions with me that he fully knew what he was doing at the time he did it, I arrived at the trial strategy of trying to play up his alluding to the movie *Clockwork Orange* and experiencing rage as a result of that movie—that maybe that would catch the jury into believing there was a temporary diminished capacity."

The prosecution, in hopes of making a case for premeditated, first-degree murder, asked Linda and Dennis to testify individually about the horrifying way they found their daughter. They agreed to do so.

On a day when Karen could have been basking in her high school graduation, her parents would take their turn sitting in the witness chair of a downtown Pittsburgh courtroom. The young man who murdered their daughter was seated not more than 25 feet away. Also in that courtroom, besides the judge, attorneys, 12 jurors, media, and array of court officials, were many sympathetic faces for the Hurwitzes—friends and family who hoped their presence might somehow lessen the pain for the grieving parents as they relived the crime of October 27.

The witness stand could only seat one, though. Each parent was alone, recalling memories that would never completely fade, never make sense, never allow for lasting peace.

"Terrible," is the word that Sandy Neiman believes best describes what it was like for the Hurwitzes. Sandy, who attended the three-day trial, particularly marveled at the courage it took for a father to be in the same room as the person who brutally betrayed his child. "Dennis testified—he showed remarkable restraint. Here he was sitting in chair almost directly across from this guy who killed his daughter!"

Mick listened passively to both Linda and Dennis speak about his friend, Karen. Eye contact was never established between the accused and either parent. Dennis, at one point in his testimony, finally did what any father in that situation would probably do. He broke down. The uncontrollable tears came not from detailing his efforts to resuscitate his daughter or from describing her gory wounds or from recalling the moment he concluded that she was dead—the tears came when he was asked to identify a small, red trinket that police had seized from Mick. Minutes later, after Dennis regained his composure, he explained that inside the inexpensive plastic keepsake was a photograph of him and his daughter that was taken during a family vacation at a nearby amusement resort.

Along with the Hurwitzes' testimony, the prosecution displayed graphic pictures of Karen's body after the murder; established the events that occurred on October 27, 1989, through the testimony of homicide detectives; and had several friends of Karen and Mick testify about the defendant's rational state of mind in the weeks and days before Karen's murder. "No one felt that he acted peculiarly different," says Dennis. The prosecution also played Mick's 32-minute tape-recorded confession for the jury.

Mr. Botula countered the case against his client with the *Clockwork Orange* defense, which included having the jury watch a portion of the motion picture. However, he didn't have an expert witness testify to support his contention. He told the city's morning newspaper, the *Pittsburgh Post-Gazette,* that in his estimation the psychiatrists and psychologists he consulted before the trial wouldn't have strengthened his case of diminished capacity. "It was a judgment call not to introduce the evidence that was presented to me, because I felt that was more damaging than helpful," the newspaper quoted him saying. His only witness was an aide at the detention center holding the defendant, who described Mick's confused state of mind. Mick didn't testify.

"The defense was just ridiculous," says Sandy, a Harvard law school graduate. "But it is presumably what the defendant said. There was never any question in my mind what was going to happen."

In Mr. Botula's closing argument, he beseeched the jurors to find his client guilty of third-degree murder, not murder one. The prosecution never provided a motive, but stressed that it was evident Mick knew what he was doing and never lost control of himself. The jury needed 80 minutes to come to a unanimous verdict.

The case and its verdict would eventually receive international notoriety in Vincent LoBrutto's book *Stanley Kubrick: A Biography (New York City: D.I. Fine): In Pittsburgh, Pennsylvania, on June 21, 1990, Michale Anderson, who had just turned 18 the day before, was convicted of stabbing 17-year-old Karen Hurwitz six times in the chest with a 36-inch martial arts sword. Anderson confessed to wearing* A Clockwork Orange *T-shirt on the day of the murder. Anderson's lawyer, Jon Botula, argued that Anderson was driven to murder by repeated viewings of the Stanley Kubrick film. As part of the defense strategy, Botula showed the jury 50 minutes of* A Clockwork Orange *to demonstrate the violence in the film. Deputy district attorney W. Christopher Conrad countered the argument, saying, "Even young Alex [the degenerate in the movie], if he saw what young Mick did, would take a lesson in 'ultra violence.' Opponents and defenders of the media argued over the notion of the power of the movies to incite violence.*

The city's afternoon newspaper, *The Pittsburgh Press*, reported that Mick accepted the guilty verdict stoically. Dennis and Linda cried. Afterward, Dennis told the media throng that the conviction will "help us go on." He added that, "Karen was with us through the whole trial. Every time we heard about her wounds, we hurt again."

Linda, wiping away tears with a tissue, preferred to talk about the daughter she remembered, trying not to speak about the daughter that was

The Chase for Beauty

killed. "She was the most nonjudgmental, most caring, thoughtful person," she told reporters. "All Karen tried to do was be a good friend." Both Dennis and Linda cautioned about being too trusting. "That is what is so scary," Linda said. "Her friends are shaken, and so are we."

Meanwhile, Mick's attorney told the media he would appeal the decision as he raised the issue of his continuance being denied.

In addition to the murder one conviction, Mick also was found guilty of stealing the Hurwitzes' 1988 Chevrolet Beretta after the murder, and charges were still pending against him for stealing Karen's credit card and making $600 worth of unauthorized charges.

At his sentencing, Michale Anderson spoke, reading a prepared statement. "I have a few things I will not say, but eventually everything I have said will come to light," he said. He also apologized to the Hurwitzes. "I'm sorry for the sorrow I have wrought upon you. I ask you see me for what I am and not for what I have done."

As far as Dennis was concerned, Mick asked for too much.

The Chase for Beauty

Chapter Fourteen

With Michale Anderson in jail for the rest of his life—barring the unlikely event of an appeal overturning the verdict—with Jeffrey Hurwitz thriving in his home, with Dennis flourishing once again as a prominent plastic surgeon, and with Linda serving as director of the Holocaust Center of Greater Pittsburgh, it seemed as if the Hurwitzes had done what the father of Oscar Ramirez and so many others who must deal with personal tragedy can't do—they were living again, not merely existing. There was one caveat, though, which Dennis expressed in a newspaper interview with *The Pittsburgh Press:*

I can't believe that a beautiful day will always be quite as beautiful, that a nice time and a joyous family event will always be quite the same, that any wedding I'm at, I will not wish it were hers.

Still, life had moved on for Dennis, Linda, and Jeffrey. But what about the *twin*?

The community that Dennis and Linda adopted nearly 15 years ago continued to rally around the couple who lost so much. Another Pittsburgh family who knew an obstetric gynecologist outside of Pittsburgh told that doctor about the Hurwitzes' plight, which led to a telephone call. The Hurwitzes were asked if they wanted another child from a mother who, after meeting with social workers, had decided not to keep her baby once he or she was born.

The gypsy made Linda say yes. "Her words were still haunting me."

Dennis needed no convincing. "I didn't want to raise another only child if I could avoid it."

By summer's end Jeffrey had a sister, Julia Rose Hurwitz, who would be in her brother's grade at school while they grew up; Linda had her twin.

"I was done," says Dennis. His Thanksgiving pledge and the gypsy's prediction had come true.

It seemed that life truly returned again for the Hurwitzes, personally and professionally. In the March 1991 national medical journal *Plastic and Reconstructive Surgery*, a letter titled *Response to Our Tragedy* was published. The author was Dennis J. Hurwitz, MD. In the letter, he stated, *the practice of plastic surgery is a remarkable privilege but a distant second in importance to our family.* He mentioned the response he and Linda received from his colleagues: *How heartening it was to hear from surgeons from around the country.* He shared his good news about his new children, Jeffrey and Julia. And he talked about today. *My patients have returned, as well as a demanding work pace. My weekly Cleft Palate Center Clinics are bittersweet, since my daughter was a barometer for many patients. I am beginning to enjoy surgery again. Conferences are stimulating, and manuscript preparation is being resumed.* In closing, he extended his appreciation to the editors of the prestigious journal for publishing his letter. *Thank you for the opportunity to update my plastic surgery associates on what is important in our lives, for so many have helped us to go forward.*

Evidently, Dennis's surgeon mentality—*I may not be right, but I'm sure*—had helped save his life, his marriage, and his family. But that same mentality wasn't faultless. The Hurwitz dream house, where he and Linda had vowed to keep living their lives, too often became the Hurwitz nightmare whenever someone opened the back door.

"It was traumatic walking out there and looking at the spot where we found Karen," says Linda. "It was making me feel creepy." Dennis had the same trepidation. Neither wanted to move, but neither could stay in a home that too often felt like something far, far different. To make their home a home again, one memory had to be destroyed.

"We had to make it different," says Dennis. Jeffrey and Julia would be the unknowing benefactors. The plan was to add an addition to the home that would give the children another room for playing, which would be on top of where their older sister made her gallant last stand.

Dennis and Linda mentioned to friends that they were thinking about building an addition to their home. All of them completely understood, and a few passed along the name of an architect who did beautiful work. The Hurwitzes made the call.

The reference didn't surprise Tony Stillson. "I have done all kinds of big buildings, but if you do somebody's kitchen in Squirrel Hill, the whole community knows your name."

The award-winning architect, who had been in practice for 25 years, was aware of the Hurwitzes' fate. "I'm not a newspaper reader, but I knew about the story of the daughter and the fact that it happened right there on the grounds. I got the sense that it was a new beginning for them. We never actually spoke about it; it was just in the air that this deal was about that."

Stillson visited the Hurwitzes at their home to view for himself what they had in mind. They talked in the den. "I remember walking into that room and feeling right, liking being there. It wasn't fashionable or stunning, but I had no sense of superficiality of the house. I've done $5 million houses where the first and second floors are strictly for show, and the family lives in the basement." That wasn't what the Hurwitzes had in mind. "I remember feeling this was going to be a worthwhile job."

There was never a mention of Karen. There was no need.

"When you are doing residential work, it's a Ouija board kind of a deal," explains Stillson. "I have to pick up on the spirit that is driving the project. Some people think it is about what brand of faucet they should buy, but it's not. It's about creating a place for important things in life to happen. My projects live well; 15 years later, I'll bump into people, and they tell me their daughter got married in the yard, and this and that. They get it. But going in, that isn't always the case."

He realized that the Hurwitzes got it: "I had absolutely no sense that this was any kind of interim house. This was where they were going to be. With them, human values were at play all the time. No one was wringing their hands over the color of the walls or to have it be at least as good as your girlfriend's. We were kind of on the same wavelength in terms of what was important. The money was spent to give space and relationship within it. It was about birthday parties for kids and cocktail parties for doctors."

The architect and Dennis got along very well. "Dennis is a very down to earth guy—all surgeons have an attitude, but Dennis did not. As a matter of fact, I was later surprised to know of his prominence. He is well known enough that if you need new boobs, you go to Dennis. If you are going to fix your nose, you go to Dennis. Turns out he has done some work on my stepdaughter."

The job kept evolving. It began as a breakfast room with a small playroom. Then, there were changes to the upstairs bedrooms, followed by a finished basement, and a new entryway.

"It was very expensive," says Linda.

For the playroom, which would now be as large as the existing den, Dennis wanted a skylight. Mr. Stillson advised against it. "He said skylights are a pain in the ass," says Dennis. "Just put in a dome ceiling. You will have plenty of light in here. He was right. You can never darken a room with skylights, and they do leak."

Mr. Stillson also convinced them to not wall off the new playroom from the kitchen. "I really didn't want it open," says Linda. "You have to realize we had Little Tikes stuff all over the place." A wall would give the kitchen some solitude, but Mr. Stillson thought that Linda would want to see her children playing. Linda acquiesced. "He said you can always a build a wall later." They didn't.

Not all the final plans came from the architect.

Dennis was concerned that the low basement roof made the room claustrophobic. He suggested they raise the foyer a step, which would

also raise the basement ceiling. Mr. Stillson embraced the creativity. The plastic surgeon, whose mother was an interior decorator, wasn't done. He discussed removing the home's second staircase to the upstairs. His wife was impressed with the idea. "Dennis had the vision to get rid of the back steps, which would give us one big entryway instead. It would create this amazing foyer, which would be fabulous."

"Tony incorporated some of my ideas," Dennis says in his typical low-key manner. "We complemented each other."

Throughout much of the construction, which took several months, the Hurwitzes, dog and all, moved to the third floor of the family home of Dennis's sister. "It was our Anne Frank attic," jokes Linda. "We had the two portable cribs. It was communal living. I like to cook and my sister-in-law, Marilyn, really doesn't. So the deal was I would do the cooking."

On weekends, the Hurwitzes would pack their bags and travel to Seven Springs Mountain Resort, which is tucked away in the Laurel Highlands, the same area where legendary architect Frank Lloyd Wright built his masterpiece home named Fallingwater.

Seven Springs is best known as a ski resort, but there is plenty to do there when there isn't snow—biking, hiking, fishing, golfing, or in the case of the Hurwitzes, escaping. They stayed in a condominium they shared with Mara Reuben and her new husband, Michael Aronson. It was the second marriage for Mara and Michael, and Mara says she and her husband bought the condominium in 1990 as a way to "bring our new families and friends together." The Hurwitzes didn't need the getaway for bonding. They needed it for a different reason.

"It was a haven for them," says Mara. "I think a wonderful way to create almost a glass wall to retreat behind, not to shut out the world, but just to retreat and heal in a different place, and then to create a whole new bank of memories with Jeffrey and Julia."

By Thanksgiving 1991, two years after Dennis made his family's declaration to look to the future, Mr. Stillson's work was complete. He was satisfied with what he accomplished. "There is a single definition to good

Chapter Fourteen

153

architecture and that is—timelessness. That is what I shoot for. I have people who call me and say, 'Thirty-two years ago I bought the house, we loved it then, we're moving out today, and we love it even more. We had a lifetime here, and it served us well. Thanks.' That is the object."

Mr. Stillson achieved his objective in the opinion of his clients. "We loved what he did," says Linda. Memories were preserved, new memories would be made, and the physical existence of one memory was purged. "We couldn't live here if it was that night we were thinking about. We think about her presence, but it's not oppressive for some reason," says Dennis. "Frankly, it's a bit of an enigma, even to me."

Although the home was finished, the weekend trips to Seven Springs continued. The retreat was needed. On December 11, 1991, the Pennsylvania Superior Court, Pittsburgh District, voted 2—1 that Michale Anderson should have an evidentiary hearing to determine if he had effective legal representation at his trial. Mick's new court-appointed attorneys claimed that Mr. Botula erred by not having expert psychiatric witnesses during the trial. In its ruling, the Superior Court stated:

If counsel is found to have been ineffective, a new trial must be granted. If counsel was not ineffective, however, the judgment of sentence may be re-imposed.

The Commonwealth sought to have the Pennsylvania Supreme Court overturn that decision, but the high court did not. As a result, the evidentiary hearing took place on February 2, 1993, in Judge Robert E. Dauer's courtroom, the same judge who oversaw the original trial. At the hearing, Mr. Botula gave his testimony that explained his *Clockwork Orange* strategy. After both sides completed their questioning of Mr. Botula, Michale Anderson testified. Public-defender attorney Shelly Stark asked her client what he thought of Mr. Botula's defense:

Anderson: "I told him [Mr. Botula] that it had no relevance to my case. I said that it wasn't true, and I said that it was, excuse me, 'bullshit.'"

Stark: "What was his response?"

Anderson: "Well, I explained why the movie came up to begin with, you know, the question of it. And I told him I was being investigated—that the police were investigating me, and one of the officers asked why I had done what they say I did. And I told him that I didn't know, but then I looked down and noticed I was wearing a *Clockwork Orange* T-shirt, and I noted the irony of it; I'm just sitting there in jail somewhere, the last place that I thought I would be, and, you know, the movie —parts of the movie happened to center on violence."

Stark: "So you thought it was ironic?"

Anderson: "Yes, I thought it was really ironic."

Stark: "But nothing to do with your acts?"

Anderson: "No, no. I just made the statement."

Stark: "And you told that to Mr. Botula?"

Anderson: "Yes, I told him it had no basis on anything."

Under cross-examination from Mr. Conrad, deputy district attorney and original prosecutor of the case, Michale Anderson was asked to read his written confession:

I loved the movie A Clockwork Orange *and every time I did anything bad, it was in my* Clockwork Orange *shirt.*

Chapter Fourteen

Anderson: "It is a shock to me."

Conrad: "So you did say that—that is your writing, isn't it?"

Anderson: "I concede that, yes."

After hearing the testimony and arguments, Judge Dauer ruled that Mr. Botula had not provided an ineffective defense. Michale Anderson's appeal was denied. The decision provided great relief for the Hurwitzes, their family, their friends, and much of the community—though most understood that all of Mick's appeal possibilities hadn't yet been exhausted. Nevertheless it was welcome news for the Hurwitzes.

Much like the 1980s—at least before October 27, 1989, the 1990s began to pick up momentum for the Hurwitzes. Jeffrey and Julia were happy, healthy well-adjusted children; Dennis and Linda remained an integral part of the Jewish philanthropic community; Linda continued to enhance the reputation of the Holocaust Center of Greater Pittsburgh; and Dennis's reputation and prominence as a plastic surgeon flourished. His chase for beauty was back in full force.

There was some more sadness, too, but at least it was a natural sadness. Both of Dennis's parents and Linda's father passed away. None ever came to grips with what happened to Karen, but at least they lived long enough to see that Dennis and Linda weren't destroyed in the aftermath. All three were buried in Pittsburgh; although for Dennis's parents, there was a bit of controversy

Dennis's mom, who had remarried after her divorce, had relocated to California. Her second husband passed away and was cremated, and Dennis says his mom wished to be cremated, also, when she died. "She said I want you to have my ashes. It seemed to her closer than a cemetery, to have her ashes in an urn nearby." Dennis wonders, though, if there was a more devious reason for her choice. "At times, I think she did things almost to irritate her son." Dennis was speaking of Shimon, whom his mom never accepted as Shimon—to her, he was always Stephen.

When Shimon heard his mother had made plans to be cremated once she died, it did more than irritate him. In his mind, it was blasphemy. Orthodox and Conservative Jews forbid cremation based, in part, on the passage in Genesis (3:19) when God tells Adam: *By the sweat of your face, will you eat bread, until you return to the ground; for out of it were you taken; you are dust, and unto dust you shall return.* To Shimon, it was of paramount importance that his mother be returned to the ground once she died if she hoped to have a place with the Creator in eternity. Knowing his mother would never listen to him, he pleaded with Dennis to change her mind. He did.

"I told her that it really makes no difference to her. 'What do you care what happens to you after you die? You don't believe in the hereafter anyhow. But he believes. You don't want to make him miserable for the rest of his life, do you? He is your son.'"

She still didn't call him Shimon, but, by agreeing to not be cremated, she acknowledged that he was still her son.

A year later, in 1996, she became terminally ill. She knew the end was near, and she knew she was going to be buried in the same cemetery as her first husband. It was her turn to make a plea to Dennis: "I want your father far away," she told her son, and explained why. "I don't want to be lying next to him. I want to be at eternal peace." Dennis chuckled at his mother's "wonderful sense of humor" even with the imminence of death. Her final resting place is in a plot next to Karen. Dennis's father, who died in 1994, is "across the road, under a tree."

To the surprise of no one, Shimon didn't attend the funeral of either parent or Dennis's father-in-law, who died in 1992.

Meanwhile, by 1994, Dennis returned full-time to the University of Pittsburgh, where he became director of the Aesthetic Plastic Surgery Center, which had a grand plan to eventually encompass a center of excellence in aesthetic plastic surgery at Magee-Womens Hospital. The center, once it became a reality, would be staffed by plastic and oral surgeons, dermatologists, ophthalmologists, and other specialists to provide cosmetic surgery, skin care, cosmetic dentistry, massage, micro pigmentation, nutrition, and fitness counseling.

His medical practice seemed to be growing exponentially from word of mouth, referrals, and publicity. His work still consisted primarily of facial cosmetic surgery with a subspecialty in cleft lip and palate craniofacial surgery, but, also, he had built a reputation for undertaking the most difficult cases from across that nation.

Success, in any field, even medicine, is never a solitary endeavor. There needs to be support—at home and at work. Dennis knew that and made sure he had both. Members of his staff weren't employees, they were his team, just as Linda, Jeffrey, and Julia were his team at home. Dennis's teammates had different backgrounds; some had already been successful, some had not. It didn't matter to Dennis. All that he cared about was their desire, their loyalty, their unselfishness, their kindness, their strength. He could teach them everything else.

Mary Manley's life had been a success. She was very attractive, the mother of three boys, a fitness instructor, and a wife. Her success came to a halt when, in her late 30s, she was no longer a wife, she was a divorcée. She had no money, no full-time career, and three teenage boys to raise. Like Dennis, she didn't give up or wallow in self-pity. She enrolled in a trade school to learn a profession. In 1994, she was qualified to be an operating room scrub technician and found full-time hospital employment. It was her job to make sure every surgical instrument was at the fingertips of the surgeon and that none mysteriously disappeared or were left behind, maybe attached to someone's gall bladder. She loved her work. The only problem was the shift. She had evenings, which began at 3 PM and didn't end until 11 PM. During the weekends, she was on call, too. The schedule was far from ideal. She wanted to be a mom to her boys, not someone who merely kept a roof over their heads and was never around when they returned home from school.

The Chase for Beauty

Perhaps it was fate or perhaps it was a coincidence, but it just so happened that around the time she was wondering how she could change her routine, she scrubbed in on an operation being performed by Dennis. The surgeon was impressed with Mary's agility and thoroughness. He needed a full-time scrub technician for his practice and thought that Mary might be one.

Never one for formal interviews, he asked Mary once the operation ended to meet with him in the doctor's hospital lounge. Once there, Mary says she couldn't stop talking. She told him that she thought liposuction shouldn't be the only way to control weight, how people need to learn more about the benefits of exercise and diet. As a fitness instructor, she recalled how she motivated some people to overcome their weight problems without surgery.

Dennis admired her spirit. He told her about the plans for the center of excellence, where exercise and nutrition would be key components.

"I thought, wow," says Mary. "This guy's high energy and a visionary person. He had this dream to have a surgery center. It sounded like he had the plans all rolled up, what he wanted to create as far as for wellness—I'm not even going to say plastic surgery—I'm just going to say for wellness in the Pittsburgh area. I liked him immediately."

Dennis liked her, too. He offered her the job while they were still seated in the lounge wearing their OR scrubs.

"It was like a godsend to me," says Mary. She accepted.

They worked very well together. "There's a chemistry between a doctor and his scrubs," says Mary. "They're right beside him in the OR, and what we do makes the flow of his day go smoothly." It didn't take long for her to marvel at his talent. "One of the big differences I saw in Dr. Hurwitz from the other surgeons is when he decides to make a cut, he makes the cut. When he does something like a facelift, he looks, he draws, and he just makes the cut. He just does it. It's incredible. He can eyeball something; he doesn't have to do all the BS things that a lot of other surgeons feel they need to do, because he just knows. He has God-given talents that a lot of people don't have. It's miraculous to watch."

She also admires his self-confidence garnished with a touch of humility, which is readily apparent when patients thank him for his work. "He tells them, 'You were terrific, and so was I,' and that's how good surgeons have to be," says Mary. "I can see how a lot of people might think of that as arrogance. Well, no, there's a fine line between competence and arrogance. Arrogance is when you can't back it up, but he can."

Mary has seen the proof when patients wait for their follow-up exams, especially his cleft palate patients whom he operated on sometimes when they were still infants. "They come back, sometimes when they're seniors in high school, and he's not in the room yet, and they'll say, 'He's changed my life.' And, he has. He's taken someone who would have looked like a freak, but who has become a beautiful teenager who leads a wonderful life."

It wasn't just his talent that impressed Mary. It was his energy. "Lots of times he would come into the office with suitcases, because as soon as he was done with his three o'clock case, he had to be on a plane. He'd have to be at the airport by 5 o'clock, because he'd be taking off for Florida or somewhere for another conference. Sometimes, when he'd come in with a suitcase, I'd say, 'Did Linda finally throw you out?' He can take our humor so well. We could just rip him, and he was so great about that; some docs in the group wouldn't like that, they'd get all PO'd.

Dennis was Mary's Renaissance man. Successful. Athletic. Witty. Charming. Generous. If she subscribed to a dating service, her ideal selection would have possessed his characteristics, except for one. He was married. Of course, that wouldn't stop some men. Dennis, she says, never once crossed the line. "That's why I like him. Because he's a man. Yeah. And Linda can trust him. He's not a creep."

For all the recollections about her boss, there is one moment that stands apart from the others. Mary vividly remembers one of the first times that she scrubbed in with him. The surgery was going well, no complications,

The Chase for Beauty

they were completely in sync. "When you're a scrub tech, you're right there with the surgeon." There was some limited conversation but mostly music, piped through the intercom, provided the background sounds.

The moment the first chords of John Lennon's song *Imagine* could be heard, Dr. Hurwitz's scalpel stopped moving, and the surgeon stepped back. Mary was surprised. She wondered if he wanted to explain something to the resident, though she knew that didn't make sense. She had already seen him talk, teach, and operate at the same time. Why then, the pause?

He turned to Mary.

"My daughter loved this song."

"Oh, you have a daughter?"

"I have two, but one died."

"Oh, I'm so sorry, Dr. Hurwitz."

"This was the first time I ever heard about Karen," says Mary. Dennis proceeded to tell her about Karen, about the murder, about the song *Imagine*. "This is how Karen thought life should be," he said. "Listen. Listen to these words."

One of the confidential rules taught to Mary during her training was to never cry in front of a doctor for any reason. She broke that rule long before the final chords of *Imagine* were heard.

"Later," Mary says, "he told me, 'Mary, no matter what happens to you, life has to go on, that's what we're here for. You're doing that, too. Your life, what was your whole life, was pulled out from you when you got divorced. You know, people that you love disappoint you or go away, and you're stuck with a big responsibility. Here you are, raising three boys on your own, and you're doing it, no matter how hard it is, you're doing it. That's what we have to do.'"

It was advice Dennis had lived by, and it was advice he would do well to remember again. The specter of returning to a courtroom was looming on the horizon—and not just from the latest Michale Anderson appeal.

Chapter Fourteen

It was entirely possible that his livelihood, his medical career that had helped so many people, was under siege.

Chapter Fifteen

From afar, Heather Lewinski seemed like a cute 8-year-old child with her blond hair and big eyes. But, even for eight-year-olds, life isn't lived from afar—not at school, not at the playground, not at the mall. Everyone began to notice. Heather had a rare skin disorder, first surfacing after a fall when she was 3 years old. It's typically called Parry-Romberg syndrome, where part of the face's skin hardens and essentially stops growing. In Heather's case, it was on the left side of her face, along the lower lip, including part of the chin and jaw line. From photographs, it looked like a pruned, purplish imprint, just to the left of the chin, as if she had been hit by a sledgehammer. The skin was just withering away.

The cause of the ailment is unknown. The younger and older brother of Heather didn't have any skin problems, nor was there any history of skin diseases in Heather's extended family. Evidently, it was just fate. A cruel fate. Heather started to see the stares, started to hear the same questions. She asked her mom why she didn't look like the other kids. Her parents, particularly her mother, started to worry that her daughter's self-esteem might begin slipping away.

Like any loving mom, Lauri Lewinski wanted to make her daughter's problem disappear or, at the very least, make sure that it didn't worsen. She and her husband, Michael, hoped and prayed that something could be done to correct Heather's disfigurement. There were doctor visits—pediatricians, dermatologists, a rheumatologist—trips to different hospitals, including the Mayo Clinic. All in search of beauty for Heather, all to end the ceaseless questions about what happened.

Was she burned?

Did something spill on her?

At one of those medical trips, Ms. Lewinski says the doctor told her they should make an appointment with Dr. Hurwitz, an expert in aesthetic facial reconstruction. She did. The family, who lived just outside of Buffalo, New York, came to Pittsburgh. Dr. Hurwitz recalls the case. The bottom left side of her face was permanently disfigured, and aside from the appearance concerns, it was causing her to drool slightly because her mouth was becoming misaligned. "No one had offered any particular surgery solution," he says.

Dr. Hurwitz examined Heather Lewinski in February 1994. He concluded that the disease was dormant and the timing was appropriate for corrective surgery. "He had all the right answers," says Ms. Lewinski, who had become the family's point person for Heather's medical care. Dr. Hurwitz believed he could help Heather through tissue expansion. It's a fairly simple procedure of placing an expander, which is like a small balloon, under the skin and then periodically inflating it with saline, causing the skin on top of the expander to protrude and expand. Once the skin was sufficiently expanded, Dr. Hurwitz would remove the expander, excise Heather's unsightly, damaged tissue, and move the expanded skin into place.

Dr. Hurwitz also recommended that the tissue expansion be completed in a timely manner. "There was no need to wait further," he explains. "In fact, with time, the contracted, lifeless skin could cause further difficulties. And Heather seemed very aware and troubled by the disease, as did her family."

The Lewinskis were impressed. There was another approach Dr. Hurwitz could have chosen, which involved inserting fat underneath the diseased skin. That procedure could bring some shape back to the area. "That was the more typical choice," says Dr. Hurwitz. But he says it wouldn't address the skin's discoloration and texture: "The skin would never look right. I felt it was too damaged."

His plan would leave scars, including some that would encircle the transfer of tissue. But, ideally, the scars would be less intrusive, especially if placed in the natural creases of the face, as opposed to the alternative of leaving Heather with a patch of darkened, prune-looking skin. He had no qualms recommending the tissue-expander option. "It's a procedure I have done from time to time when I am taking out birth defects," he says.

The approach made sense to Ms. Lewinski, but she did go for other opinions. None offered a better option. "I wasn't real thrilled with some of the things they [the other doctors] were saying," she says. None of them, she recalls, questioned Dr. Hurwitz's approach or made her ask herself, *Wait a minute, why is Dr. Hurwitz so enthusiastic and upbeat about this, verses this doctor saying, "This is a very rare condition."*

"I mean, I knew it was a rare condition," says Ms. Lewinski. "Nobody was contradicting him, I guess."

In terms of any downside concerning the operation, Ms. Lewinski says neither Dr. Hurwitz nor anyone else mentioned anything out of the ordinary. "It was your usual stuff," says Ms. Lewinski, citing cautions about possible infection, general anesthesia, "the normal stuff that if you went to get a gallbladder removed. Certainly nothing that would raise a red flag in any way."

And, if all went well, Ms. Lewinski says the renowned Pittsburgh plastic surgeon explained there would only be a small scar along the nasolabial fold, which is the natural crease that goes from a person's nose to the corner of the lip.

Ms. Lewinski signed the consent forms for the first of the surgeries, and, on May 4, 1994, Dr. Hurwitz inserted a tissue expander in Heather's cheek and neck to expand healthy skin. All seemed to go as planned. "It was just part of this little pillow underneath the skin," says Ms. Lewinski. She, like Dr. Hurwitz, was upbeat until a troublesome development occurred.

Chapter Fifteen

The tissue expansion was painful to Heather, especially when she received regular injections of saline to inflate the tissue expanders and cause the skin to stretch. "It was painful as hell," says Ms. Lewinski. "[Dr. Hurwitz] had it set up with a woman here in Buffalo, and the day she would inject, Heather would be down; if she moved, it would hurt. She was down that entire day, basically sleeping all day, as it was painful."

Then came another troublesome development. Infection set in within the first month of the expansion. In order to ward off escalation of the infection, Dr. Hurwitz reduced the tissue expansion timeline from 12—16 weeks to seven weeks. At seven weeks, he measured how much the skin had expanded and, after doing so, he felt confident about moving forward.

"He took this little ruler thing with a slide thing on it, did a pinch measure and said, we've got enough skin. We're ready to go," Ms. Lewinski stated. "I just thought, her skin has stretched well, we moved along quick, awesome, let's get this out."

Had Dr. Hurwitz deduced that there was not enough expanded tissue to work with, he would have been forced to start the tissue expansion again, knowing that would have meant more pain for Heather. Dr. Hurwitz questioned to himself about whether his young patient would have the fortitude to undergo the same expansion procedure a second time. Fortunately for Heather, she wouldn't face that predicament. "I felt I had enough skin," says Dr. Hurwitz.

The next surgical step involved removing the expanders, cutting out the atrophied skin, and covering the area with the newly expanded skin. More consent forms signed. More surgery. That reconstruction operation took place on June 27, 1994.

The next day, when the bandages were removed, Ms. Lewinski was shocked by what she saw. "I thought, 'Oh my God, what did he do?' That was my initial reaction—she had scars down the lip, by the nose, all the way down in the middle of her face, all the way around her lip, down the center of her chin, and all the way up to her ear. I said to the doctor that was there taking out the drain, 'What is this?' He looked dumbfounded and said, 'What do you mean?' I said, 'Geez, this isn't what I bargained for. What is this?' He referred me back to Dr. Hurwitz."

She says Dr. Hurwitz told her not to worry. "He just kept telling me, 'It will be all right. With plastics, it gets worse before it gets better. Give it six months.'"

Dr. Hurwitz recalls Ms. Lewinski's dismay. "I understand that a mother, upon seeing the immediate result of her child, would be distressed," he says, "It's never a welcome site to see a series of scars put on a face in reconstructive surgery, and there is no way to adequately prepare a mother for that. But I'm not sure why that was such a mystery to her, because I pretty much outlined them. There would be scars where the flaps came from—one above, one below—and there would be scars where they were being inset. Actually, the initial incision lines were very fine, exactly what I planned."

During the next six months, Ms. Lewinski says she had a few telephone conversations with Dr. Hurwitz. "I was like waiting for this miraculous event to occur," she says, "and it never occurred." What she was waiting for, says Dr. Hurwitz, was for the scars to settle down: "Early on, the scars typically swell and thicken, usually within the first month, but in six months or so the scars will mature— they will thin down, become less red, less obtrusive as part of the healing process."

While waiting for that to happen, another problem developed. Heather's lower lip was being pulled downward on the left side, which caused her to drool more significantly than before the operation. The embarrassment for Heather was indescribable, says Ms. Lewinski. It had to be fixed. Dr. Hurwitz agreed. To do so, she says Dr. Hurwitz wanted to insert another tissue expander to create skin for making a correction. Originally, there had been enough expanded skin, says Dr. Hurwitz, but afterward the skin contracted slightly, in part from some unforeseen excessive scarring. The tension from the contracted, tightened skin pulled the lip down slightly as if Heather had suffered a mild stroke.

Ms. Lewinski gave Dr. Hurwitz the okay for the corrective procedure. In September 1995, expanders were again inserted in Heather's face. They were a different design and, fortunately for Heather, proved to be less painful. Two months later, once the skin had sufficiently expanded, Dr. Hurwitz added more skin to the damaged area to minimize the drooping lip and to re-suture the scars so they wouldn't be so prominent.

A few months afterwards, Ms. Lewinski was far from pleased with the result. The lip was still drooping, and the scars' visibility had not yet lessened. Dr. Hurwitz wasn't satisfied, either. He had hoped for better initial results, but he also knew that the healing process was still under way. After four months passed, he asked Ms. Lewinski to bring Heather back to Pittsburgh for further consultation. Ms. Lewinski remembers her reaction:

"What are we going to do now?"

"I'm going to bring some other people in"

"No, I'm going to see what people here say."

Ms. Lewinski says Dr. Hurwitz agreed. "He was really upbeat at first, you know, 'opinions are good, the more people we talk to—.'" Ms. Lewinski, on the other hand, had started to lose faith in the plastic surgeon, which prompted her to seek the opinions of others. She made an appointment with an oral surgeon in Buffalo. After the examination, Ms. Lewinski says he told her, "You need to go to this guy in Boston. He is the guru of Romberg disease. He has research money in it and is an oral surgeon."

"Okay, let's see what he has to say," Ms. Lewinski remembers thinking. She says she was ready for another opinion. The Lewinskis headed to Boston for an appointment with Dr. Leonard B. Kabin. It was in late May 1996. Heather had just celebrated her 11th birthday.

"We had four doctors in the room," says Ms. Lewinski. Dr. Hurwitz was 600 miles away. "The first doctor walked in and goes, 'What the hell did he do to her?' I stood there, and I initially thought I was going to throw up." She started to cry. "And the doctor goes, 'What the hell did you do?' And I said, 'Who?' And that's when he said, 'Hurwitz' and I'm like, 'Oh my God.' You know how doctors talk around you, but not to you? They were talking to one another. 'Well, maybe we could do this, and maybe —,' and I said, 'Oh my God.'

"I knew with the discussion they were having amongst the four of them, we were at the point of no return, and I knew things would never— I knew I couldn't turn the clock back. And they quite clearly described that, they just basically said, 'In Romberg disease it's a stuffing thing, you put stuff under the skin; he excised skin. We will never be able to give that back to her. He had taken a piece out of her lip, you can never put that back.' They were very, very clear that they could not correct what he had done."

There was one more telephone call to Dr. Hurwitz. She told him about the consultation in Boston and that she lost all confidence in him. He tried to voice his opinion, but she says she wouldn't let him. "I hung up on him."

The next time Dr. Hurwitz spoke to Ms. Lewinski about Heather, it would be through the attorney representing her family.

The threat of a lawsuit concerned Dr. Hurwitz, but he remained steadfast in his conviction that he did nothing improper: "I felt that I executed her surgery in a very effective and conscientious way and for lack of excessive scarring, and the pulling and contraction, it would have been all right. I had taken out the disease and no new disease occurred."

But there was excessive scarring that led to the pulling and skin contraction. "Like anything," he says, "Monday morning quarterbacking is easy after the game is lost. She had a problem, and there were a number of ways that it could have been done differently, and I was particularly vulnerable because the approach I used in trying to give Heather the best possible result was construed by some as unorthodox. But it wasn't. I was using known techniques, applied in an innovative way. There is a difference. What becomes standard of care, much of what is standard of care right now, must first be innovative. Did I get the result I hoped for, that the Lewinskis hoped for? No! Did I in any way violate my standard of care for Heather? No way! What was lost with Heather's parents was that this was a young girl who already was going to be disfigured for the rest of her life. I was the one who tried to help her."

When it came to courtrooms, Dennis had what he considered a much more pressing concern. On September 27, 1996, the Superior Court of Pennsylvania vacated the judgment of Michale Anderson's 1993 evidentiary hearing, in which his lawyers claimed that he received an inadequate defense during his 1990 trial. His new counsel asserted that his intent to murder Karen and steal the Hurwitzes' car was significantly impaired by his bipolar disorder. Affidavits from two psychiatrists now substantiated that claim. The Superior Court upheld the appeal and ordered a new murder trial. The presiding district attorney's office did appeal the Superior Court ruling, but it was denied. There would be a new trial

For Dennis and Linda, for their family and their friends, it meant the unthinkable—reliving Karen's murder once more. "It's bizarre," Dennis was quoted as saying in the *Pittsburgh Post-Gazette*. "He is a confessed murderer. There is no new evidence. Why are the taxpayers having to pay for this?"

There was something new, though. Dr. Gary Vallano, a psychiatrist who interviewed the defendant at the Shuman Youth Detention Center soon after the killing, and Dr. Robert Wettstein, a local psychiatrist who examined Mick as part of the appeals process, were both willing to testify that Mick was diagnosed with bipolar disorder and unable to formulate the premeditated criminal intent necessary to warrant a first-degree murder conviction. If the jury agreed, Mick's sentence would be reduced to either third-degree murder or voluntary manslaughter. Should that happen, it was entirely possible that at trial's end the confessed killer of Karen Hurwitz would walk away a free man for time already served.

The prosecutors did their best to assure the Hurwitzes that wasn't about to happen. The district attorney's office hired one of the nation's foremost psychiatrists in criminal casework, Dr. Michael Welner, in hopes that his findings would rebut the defense's psychiatric witnesses.

The new trial would begin on June 8, 1998. For Dennis and Linda, it would mean testifying once more about October 27, 1989, a day that they were spending the rest of their lives trying to forget. It would mean looking again at the gruesome pictures of Karen's death, and, perhaps most inconceivable, it would mean again calmly sitting in the same room with their daughter's confessed killer.

"I was thinking about how can I just sit there and not just lay into him," says Dennis. "I really wanted to hit this punk. I really wanted to do it. But I kept telling myself that I have to have faith in the judicial system."

For Linda, the thought of seeing Mick again made her think of her deceased father who, at the hands of Nazis, lost his first wife and family in World War II and who came perilously close to dying in a concentration camp in Germany. "I remembered my father's words," says Linda. "He said to me that when he was liberated from the concentration camp, he could have picked up a gun or beat a Nazi, and he would have been totally justified. But he couldn't act that way.

"So, it was in my head, too—that my father, what he had seen and lived through was unbelievable, but he still acted as a dignified human being. It does go through your mind, 'Why am I being so rational? I don't feel like being rational,' but if you let yourself act on violent impulses, you are, in a way, admitting you could be what they are, and then it confuses the whole issue about who is the good guy and who is the bad guy. So, you try to retain your dignity in the face of everything."

When a handcuffed Michale Anderson entered the courtroom, by all accounts with a confident stride, Dennis and Linda did their best to maintain their dignity and their belief in the judicial system. For Mick, the moment was a chance, perhaps his last, at freedom. When he caught a glimpse of the Hurwitzes, his first inclination was to smile at them "as an old friend." He says it was a spontaneous reaction, and he did so for just a moment. Linda didn't notice. Her eyes filled with tears at the sight of the defendant, but she remained composed otherwise. Mick believes Dennis saw his friendly glance. He says Karen's father scowled back at him, and that was the end of the eye contact for the remainder of the trial. Michael says he can understand why the Hurwitzes hate him. "I was ashamed of myself," he admits. But he didn't believe his life sentence without parole was just.

The *Pittsburgh Post-Gazette* quoted Linda as being "nervous," "anxious," and "furious" as the trial began. When the judge gave the jurors their instructions that the defendant is "presumed innocent" under the law, Dennis remained stoic, but Linda, and many of the Hurwitzes' friends who were in the courtroom, visibly recoiled.

"You don't think we freaked?" says Roz, who sat beside Linda in the first row. Roz had put her real estate clients on hold to attend the trial just as her husband, Sandy, halted his legal work. "We promised to be there every second," says Roz. "Sandy and I couldn't believe this was happening. It was worse than the first trial. The first trial we were in shock. The second trial we had our wits about us. Linda and I were just sitting there digging our hands into each other's legs."

It was clear that this trial wasn't just about Mick's fate. It was about the fate of the Hurwitzes, too, and to some extent the legacy of Karen. This potential rewriting of history should never have been given the chance to happen in Sandy's estimation. The Harvard Law graduate emphatically says that in no way was a new trial warranted. "That defense was conjured up," he says bluntly. He holds one of the defense's psychiatrists directly accountable for the retrial being granted. That psychiatrist was Dr. Wettstein, the one brought in by the defense during the appeals process. He happened to be an acquaintance of the Neimans. "He testified that Michale Anderson had this condition, but that he was still able to do the things that would have been inconsistent with the condition," recalls Sandy. "Somebody with his experience and credentials had to know that this couldn't have been the case. It was clearly his support of his psychiatric diagnosis that was at the heart of the success of the appeal. That, in turn, means that he, for what I believe were strictly mercenary reasons, caused my friends

The Chase for Beauty

to have incredible distress. I came to hate him, which I told him."

Roz recalls that confrontation; it was at an informal get-together among several couples:

"He went over to Sandy and said, 'Hi, how are you doing?'"

"Get away from me!" Sandy replied emphatically. "Don't you ever come near me! You sold out my friends. Don't you ever—"

Roz watched her former friend "run away" from her husband. She supported Sandy's actions. "I snub him [Dr. Wettstein], too, when I see him. It was disgusting what he did."

Dr. Welner, in an analytical assessment of the case, indirectly gives credence to Sandy's bitter accusations: "If someone takes a 180-degree position that is different than mine, who happens to be a colleague, either he has far less information available to him based on the work he put into the case, or he is just outright lying. Psychiatry is a consistent science and is interpreted based on standards. Two people can't interpret the same standard different ways or it is not a standard."

Dr. Welner—a New York University School of Medicine clinical associate professor in the Department of Psychiatry who had testified as an expert witness at trials in 25 states—didn't come to his conclusion on Mick quickly or inevitably. There have been cases where he has been brought in as an expert but, after completing his research and interviews, he has withdrawn from the case because his findings differed from what the prosecution expected.

Before offering his opinion on Mick, he reviewed all of the records attached to the case, including police reports, corrections records, psychiatric reports—most notably those of doctors who believed Mick was mentally ill. Afterward, he talked to witnesses, and then he met with Mick for 10 hours of face-to-face interviews. "You have to go into it with a completely open mind," Dr. Welner says, "because it is an adversarial system. If there is one flaw in my conclusions, then the opposing attorney will expose me in court, and the flaws of my work will be exposed and widely known to anyone who researches me in a subsequent case. Your reputation is either protected or destroyed in every single case."

In the Michale Anderson case, Dr. Welner was confident his reputation would remain intact.

"What often happens in flawed mental health examinations," explains Dr. Welner, "is that examiners doing the work only interview the person who is on trial and get a small portion of the information available. They draw their conclusions from that and, therefore, leave themselves open to the possibility that additional information will come up [at trial] and completely disprove how a defendant represents himself, especially because the defendant wants to appear as sick as possible in order to help his case, as was the case with Michale Anderson. The only way around that is to leave yourself open to every piece of information you can possibly get about someone, whether it comes from the defense, prosecution, or [wherever]."

In his assessment of Michale Anderson, he listed 70 sources of information, including, among others, his interviews with the defendant, the Hurwitzes, and Mick's former girlfriends and friends.

Once he had completed his analysis, he had no trouble reaching a conclusion. "The mental health evidence was really not a close call," he concluded. "I think he [Michale Anderson] personally had problems, but whether he had a mental disorder, in this case bipolar disorder, I really took issue with that and just felt that the record was quite unimpressive and it wasn't especially challenging to come to an ultimate conclusion that he did not have a major psychiatric illness. Now, granted, all of those stones had to be unturned."

Here is what he found when he unturned those stones. Mick behaved in a rational manner leading up to the killing, and he interacted with friends, none of whom identified symptoms that would enable the defense psychiatrists to support the bipolar diagnosis. "It was how unremarkable he was, relevant to how serious the defense portrayed his diagnosis, that led me to the conclusion that it just wasn't there," Dr. Welner explains.

"They were trying to say he was suffering from some sort of psychotic condition in all of the time preceding his attacking Karen. There weren't any signs of disorganization. In order to embrace that theory, you would have to phrase this as some sort of clap-on, clap-off [state of mind], all of a sudden he is insane, and all of a sudden he is no longer insane."

Dr. Welner says that when he went to the crime scene he was able to witness Mick's state of mind moments after the killing. The clue didn't come from the backyard where the killing took place. It came from the sunken driveway, which is L-shaped and is banked on either side by the yard. When Mick backed out the car from the garage after the killing, he had to navigate his way, in reverse, along the driveway.

"I measured the width of the driveway relative to the car. If he were disorganized in exiting the crime scene, he would have scraped that car. That is not an easy driveway to navigate for an inexperienced driver. He exited the driveway without incident and then calmly made his way through Squirrel Hill. What we would expect, as psychiatrists, is a period of deterioration—someone that is clearly becoming more disorganized and, at that time, doing a variety of bizarre things, and also showing these specific signs that are associated with the specific illness in question or another illness." Dr. Welner says he found no such behavior.

Dr. Wettstein, in his testimony, disagreed. He told those in the courtroom that Mick had "lost touch with reality" before killing his friend in the backyard of her home. He said Mick experienced hallucinations and "perceptual distortions" that distracted him and interfered with his ability to form an intent to kill Karen Hurwitz, which is necessary for a murder one conviction.

Dr. Welner rebutted Dr. Wettstein's findings by testifying that "mental illness is not a clap-on, clap-off phenomenon." He added that even if Mick had a bipolar condition, which he disputed, it doesn't cause people to commit unprovoked violent acts. "They aren't predatory. They don't attack a defenseless person."

Chapter Fifteen

Like the first trial, Michale Anderson chose not to testify in his own defense, while Dennis and Linda took the stand and did what their friends had prayed they wouldn't have to do. They went back in time to October 27, 1989. They did so with pain, with tears, but with a resolve that their account must be told, so Karen's killer would not go free.

Before the jurors began deliberations, the judge gave them legal instructions: Michale Anderson could not be convicted of first-degree murder unless he was in control of his actions. The verdict apparently rested on the credibility of Dr. Wettstein versus Dr. Welner.

Roz wouldn't allow herself to entertain the notion that Michale Anderson's murder one conviction could be overturned. "I remember driving with Jeffrey and Julia in the backseat of my car. Jeffrey says there is a bad man in jail, and he is going to come out and kill us. I slammed on the brakes and pulled over to the side of the road. I took them in my arms and said, 'Listen you two, nobody is going to hurt you. Not ever. You have people watching you every minute. No one is going to hurt you. That man is never getting out of jail.'"

Roz was correct. At 9 PM on Friday, June 12, 1998, after a weeklong trial, and three hours of deliberations, a second jury pronounced Mick guilty of first-degree murder, which carries an automatic life sentence with no parole. It was a moment of elation for all of the family and friends of the Hurwitzes. "I think that is accurate," says Roz, who was not at all sympathetic that the ruling meant Michale Anderson would never experience freedom again. "Obviously, it was relief, but it was definitely elation as well that this guy was not going to get out on some technicality or some conjured up medical condition. My friends could feel secure that they weren't going to have to run into this guy some day."

Dennis and Linda embraced and wept immediately after the verdict was announced. Mick, given the opportunity to speak, thanked the jurors and, before being led away in shackles, he said, "I'm sorry to the Hurwitz family for anything and everything."

The Chase for Beauty

Dr. Welner was not in the courtroom for the verdict, but the seemingly heartfelt apology from the defendant is not a surprise to him. "I would say that probably the most remarkable thing about Michale Anderson is that he did not strike me as a particularly menacing individual—but most killers don't. Killing is not a state of mind. It is a mistake a number of people make. A mistake they cannot undo. They make that mistake for all kinds of reasons, but very often, as in Michale Anderson's case, they make that mistake by choice."

For Dennis and Linda, Mick's apology didn't for a moment mask what he had done to their daughter. Reporters clamored around them outside the courtroom for their reaction to the verdict. As reported in the *Pittsburgh Post-Gazette*, Dennis said: "[We have] a sense of relief that justice is done, and this man who is evil and psychopathic will never terrorize this community again."

His comments were followed by Linda, who while wiping away tears with a tissue, reminded everyone of one harsh reality: "My daughter isn't coming back. He [Michale] still has his life."

Dennis and Linda had to try and move forward one more time as they walked down the courtroom steps. The trial had put their lives on hold again. Aside from the mental anguish, Linda, still the director of the Holocaust Center of Greater Pittsburgh, had to miss the annual national meeting of the Association of Holocaust Organizations. Dennis was affected professionally, too. There was a regional plastic surgeons meeting taking place the day after the verdict at Nemacolin Woodlands Resort, not too far from Fallingwater in the Laurel Highlands. Had it not been for the trial, Dennis definitely would have attended. It was understandable, though, that after the weeklong trial and the emotional verdict, he would be a no-show. He was drained. So was Linda. Even Jeffrey and Julia, still too young to fully understand what was going on, weren't themselves.

But Dennis wasn't about to sit around and let Michale Anderson dictate their fate. "After the verdict, he piled the kids and me in the car and we were driving through the mountains at midnight getting to Nemacolin," says Linda. It turns out, Dennis didn't miss his meeting.

At least now, it seemed that Michale Anderson was out of the Hurwit-zes' lives forever. The same was not true for the Lewinskis.

Chapter Sixteen

On January 12, 1999, 11 days before the inauguration of Dennis Hurwitz as president of the Allegheny County Medical Society, Dr. John B. Mulliken, a plastic surgeon, wrote a letter to medical malpractice attorney John P. Gismondi. It was cosigned by his colleague, Dr. Leonard B. Kaban, an oral surgeon. They were two of the doctors in the room when Lauri Lewinski took her daughter to Boston in 1996.

The letter from the associate professor of surgery at Brigham and Women's Hospital, in partnership with Harvard University, had been long awaited by Mr. Gismondi. He was representing Heather in a malpractice suit against Dr. Hurwitz.

The idea to contact an attorney had come from Dr. Kaban. When Heather's new treating physicians from Brigham and Women's Hospital were recommending more operations—it would total six during the next four years—some would not be covered by insurance.

"Oh, my God," Ms. Lewinski remembers thinking. "How much is all this going to cost? We are talking huge amounts of money here." Her husband was an electrician and earned a respectable living for the family, but by no means were the Lewinskis affluent. Dr. Kaban had some advice, says Ms. Lewinski: "I think you might want to consult an attorney." She did. Her jeweler, who knew the situation with Heather, recommended her brother-in-law, who was a lawyer living in Philadelphia. Ms. Lewinski made the call.

"He wasn't what you call an ambulance chaser," says Ms. Lewinski. She sent him all the medical records she had and talked with him numerous times on the telephone. He was interested in the case but told Ms.

Lewinski that it should really be handled by an attorney who practiced law in Pittsburgh, where the case would be tried. That's what initiated Mr. Gismondi's involvement with the Lewinskis.

"He [Ms. Lewinski's initial attorney] did some research to find whom he would regard as top-flight malpractice lawyers in Pittsburgh," says Mr. Gismondi, "and he got in touch with me. I didn't know him at all."

Mr. Gismondi didn't know Dr. Hurwitz, either. "I certainly was familiar with the name because of the case involving his daughter, but I had never met him, never had any claims against him or legal cases with him." Unlike Pittsburgh architect Tony Stillson, Mr. Gismondi had no idea if Dr. Hurwitz was considered a good surgeon or a bad surgeon.

From a legal standpoint, though, he believed the Lewinski case had potential. "I knew it was a serious situation, because any time you are talking about facial scarring, on a female and a young female, that it is a very serious situation. I knew that from the start, but I didn't know certainly in the beginning whether it was a case that had merit or didn't have merit.

"For every 25 people who call me and say, 'Hey, I think I have a lawsuit. Will you take my case against this doctor?' 24 of them get turned down probably. So you are talking about a small percentage of cases that we even accept because we do a lot of self-screening—for a variety of reasons. A lot of times, cases are refused because it may have been a bad result, but it doesn't mean it was bad medicine. And a bad result doesn't equal bad medicine. Sometimes there was bad medicine, but unfortunately litigation has become so expensive that the harm the patient suffered is not enough to support the case. There are any number of legitimate cases that never see the light of day, because, unfortunately, they are too expensive to litigate, relative to the harm suffered by the person."

To figure out whether the case had merit in a court of law meant research. "Hundreds of man-hours," says Mr. Gismondi, "long, long process." All this was done before meeting Heather in person. They did finally meet in Mr. Gismondi's downtown Pittsburgh law office.

"I remember the day she came in," he says. "I went to the waiting room and she was seated in a chair out there, and, as I approached her, she was seated with her face at an angle where I could see her profile." It was the side of her face that didn't have the disease. When Heather stood up, the profile vanished. "I was just immediately shocked by the difference between one side of her face and the other."

While he had seen the deformity in photographs, he wasn't prepared for the contrast. After he had a lengthy meeting with her and her mother, he had a conversation with his law partner. "You can't believe how pretty this girl is when you look at her from one side," he said to him. "My heart just went out to her," says Mr. Gismondi.

Coincidentally, Dr. Hurwitz had very much the same reaction when he first met Heather. He was also struck by how the disfigurement seemed to traumatize his young patient. "It's unusual for children with any kind of facial disfigurement to wish to have multistage surgery with the anticipation of pain, but she was eager to move forward, as was her mother, so obviously this was something bearing heavily on Heather. I wasn't just listening to Mom. I could feel for Heather, as I had for hundreds of other children with birth defects who were fed up with the ridicule and the unwanted attention."

As sympathetic as Mr. Gismondi felt toward the young girl, he still wasn't sure if the case had merit. That started to change after a telephone conversation with Dr. Mulliken, one of the plastic surgeons who had taken over her treatment. "It took awhile to get him on the phone," says Mr. Gismondi. He was aware that Dr. Mulliken was an acquaintance of Dr. Hurwitz, primarily through medical meetings. "Understandably, he was a little reluctant to talk to me, but eventually he did and spoke candidly; and it was once I had that initial conversation on the phone, where we were discussing the merits of the case, that I felt that we had good grounds."

Mr. Gismondi needed Dr. Mulliken to reiterate his opinion in a formal written letter. He did so. Hence, the letter, which came more than five years after Dr. Hurwitz last treated Heather:

1/12/99

Dear Mr. Gismondi,

This young lady was brought to me in 1995 [sic: i.e., 1996] by my colleague Dr. Leonard B. Kaban. She has Romberg disease, an uncommon disorder of unknown etiology that is characterized by progressive loss of facial subcutaneous tissue in childhood. The pattern usually follows one or more of the trigeminal nerve dermatome. She has had surgical procedures by Dr. Dennis Hurwitz, in an effort to correct or repair the "hemifacial atrophy."

I am usually reluctant to criticize the work of another plastic surgeon. However, it is my opinion that the thought processes and operative strategy used by Dr. Hurwitz were unconventional and not consistent with the standards of good practice.

...

He had written the magic words for a malpractice attorney—*not consistent with the standards of good practice.* "I remember that as being a critical moment," says Mr. Gismondi. He expected a settlement negotiation to begin with Dr. Hurwitz's attorney shortly thereafter. "Most every case has a price," says Mr. Gismondi, and this was no exception. "Frankly I thought they should have settled the case." He estimates that less than a quarter of his cases ultimately go to trial once he decides there is enough merit to accept and move forward.

There was no offer to settle, though, at least not with any settlement offer that Mr. Gismondi says was going to attract any interest. Just like the Lewinskis discovered when they first met with Dr. Hurwitz, Mr. Gismondi learned that his client's former doctor was not a man that walks away from a challenge.

In Dr. Hurwitz's mind, he had done nothing wrong despite Dr. Mulliken's position. One of the characteristics of plastic surgery is to take known procedures, such as tissue expanders, and apply it to another part of the body. "It happens all the time," says Dr. Hurwitz. And it happened with Heather Lewinski. There is no medical book that states unequivocally there is one and only one way to treat Heather Lewinski's rare condition.

Dr. Hurwitz does recall talk of a settlement. "My lawyer said, 'They want to settle for the maximum of your insurance, $1 million. Do you want to do that?'"

"Do you think we can win this thing?" asked Dr. Hurwitz.

"Yeah, I think we can win it, but it will be an uphill battle."

Dennis chose to do battle, whether it was taking on Parry-Romberg syndrome or taking on the Lewinskis in court.

Meanwhile, it was business as usual for Dennis, which meant squeezing every second out of every day—taking care of patients; finalizing plans for the University of Pittsburgh's multimillion dollar Aesthetic Plastic Surgery Center, which he would direct; overseeing the Allegheny County Medical Society; collaborating with University of Pittsburgh bariatric surgeon Philip Schauer on formerly obese patients who encountered problems with excess skin; and, of course, being a husband to Linda and a father to Jeffrey and Julia. His pace didn't correspond with a man in his mid-fifties. There were telltale signs of his age, though. Dennis, in his own search for beauty, noticed them every time he was interviewed or featured on television for his expertise in plastic surgery. The eyes. The cheeks. They didn't look like he felt. "I wanted to look my energy level," he says, as he anticipated a growing presence on television spotlighting his accomplishments in the field. There was a solution. It would involve fat injections to the face and some eyelid tightening. In May 2000, while in New York City, the renowned plastic surgeon experienced the operating room from a new perspective. He was on the operating table while two Manhattan plastic surgeons worked simultaneously on their friend—Sydney Coleman, whom Dennis calls "the world's authority on adding fat to the face" and Barry Zide, "a surgical innovator of the eyelids," according to Dennis.

Linda had no idea what was going on with her husband. "I was taking 28 people to Poland for the Holocaust Center, and he was supposed to be home watching the kids! Suddenly, my mother was watching them, and he went off to New York to get something done with his face."

A few days later, he was on an airplane coming home. "I was swollen like a tomato."

His appearance didn't cause him to neglect his duties with the medical society. The society's executive director, John Krah, is a strong supporter of Dennis. Mr. Krah says Dennis's outstanding reputation as a physician and his ability to "speak for medicine" to the media made him the ideal leader for articulating the society's message. "We have a mission statement that is a little longer, but my shorthand for it is that we help physicians care for patients," says Mr. Krah. "If we do what is in the best interest of patient care, we are doing what is in the best interest of physicians."

Dennis took his duties so seriously that he wasn't going to let plastic surgery keep him from one of the society's executive committee board meetings, which he helped direct. Five days after his New York City operation, he walked into the society's conference room. He had sunglasses on, and his face was extremely puffy and bruised. Mr. Krah says he was immediately alarmed:

"Oh my God! Dennis, are you all right? What happened?" He was concerned Dennis had been in a car accident. "That is what he looked like."

The other dozen or so people in the room were staring at him, too, with the same concerns.

"Well," Dennis told everyone somewhat sheepishly, "I took some of my own advice." He then proceeded to take off his sunglasses and show off his two black eyes.

"He was really swollen," says Mr. Krah. "I was shocked that he came to the meeting in that condition. It's an interesting psychology when you think about it. People have those kinds of procedures so they look different, but they don't want anybody to know, they won't admit it, and they

The Chase for Beauty

don't want it to be obvious." Not Dennis. "I think he decided, 'I did what I did, and that is that.' It spoke volumes about him being upfront."

It also showed that he was tough. There were certainly no cracks in his armor as the Lewinski trial neared. He was not going to be the first one to blink, not even after learning that Mr. Gismondi secured another medical opinion that supported Dr. Mulliken's contention. The critic was Dr. Arnold Breitbart, an assistant professor of clinical surgery at Columbia Presbyterian Center in New York. He had trained with Dr. John Siebert, who was considered an expert in Parry-Romberg syndrome. Like Dr. Mulliken, he agreed to express his opinion in writing:

1/22/01

Dear Mr. Gismondi,

I have reviewed the medical records and photographs which you forwarded me on Heather Lewinski....

It is my opinion that the care given by Dr. Hurwitz was not consistent with the standard of care for Romberg's hemifacial atrophy....

Of course, Dr. Hurwitz had colleagues who agreed with his treatment, including Dr. Donald Mackay, an associate professor of surgery and pediatrics at Penn State's College of Medicine and chief of the school's center for soft tissue expansion.

3/27/01

....I have read Dr. Mulliken's and Dr Breitbart's report.... Dr. Hurwitz's experience is typical for this type of practice. He is not only well trained, but considered an expert in aesthetic facial reconstruction. He is completely familiar with the principles and practice of tissue expansion. In my opinion, based on the photographs, there was a significant improvement in Miss Lewinski's condition after Dr. Hurwitz initially completed her flap advancements. The atrophic discolored skin had been removed and cov-

Chapter Sixteen

ered with adjacent expanded skin. She needed ongoing treatment as she grew. This would have been true regardless of who treated her.

As it turned out, the pending lawsuit wasn't the only stress, perhaps not even the primary stress, in Dennis's life. In 2000, the University of Pittsburgh, which was in the process of hiring a new chair of surgery, suddenly withdrew its support of the Aesthetic Plastic Surgery Center despite the years of planning and the countless hours devoted to it by Dennis and others. It was a devastating professional blow to Dennis. The proposed center had been what convinced him to leave his private practice in 1994 and return to the university as the center's director.

"I never got a direct answer why they canned it, but the sense was that they didn't want to go too far with such a thing without a new chairman of surgery on board to work it out," he recalls. "They took away my dream."

They took away more than that. Once the new chair of surgery was on board, he instituted some cost-cutting measures that included reducing Dennis's salary by one-third.

"That was a kick in the pants," he says. No center. Less income. No reasonable explanations. "I said to myself, 'Why am I here?'"

He wouldn't be for much longer. He decided to return to private practice in March 2001, two months before the Lewinski trial.

Some might have questioned his timing. Losing a malpractice case isn't an ideal way to attract new patients. But Dennis knew the facts of the case. He didn't expect to lose. Neither did Mr. Gismondi.

Chapter Seventeen

By all accounts, the trial went very well on behalf of the Lewinskis, even in the opinion of the judge, Alan S. Penkower. When the plaintiffs rested their case, the judge had Dr. Hurwitz's lawyer, John Bass, approach the bench before beginning his defense. He confidentially offered the attorney a few words of advice. Mr. Bass repeated to his client what the judge said: "I think you ought to go over to Mr. Gismondi and talk about settling. You're going to lose this case."

There was no question that the Lewinskis' malpractice attorney had painted a believable picture to the jury of what happened: "I think most surgeons, like most good trial attorneys, have a healthy ego," says Mr. Gismondi, who is just a few years younger than Dr. Hurwitz, trim from regular workouts at a downtown health club, and always impeccably dressed in expensive-looking suits while in the courtroom or in his office. "I think [Dr. Hurwitz] oversold his qualifications. It's one thing to puff a little bit, but when you are talking about taking an 8-year-old girl under the knife for a surgery that really, for this particular condition, nobody else has ever done—to me, above all else in this case, I think that is what hit home with the jury. That, here you are, I used the phrase in my closing argument—guinea pig—you are pretty much subjecting an 8-year-old to a surgery where nobody else has employed this strategy or this technique for this condition before, and the parents aren't aware of that. Now, that shouldn't happen."

Dr. Hurwitz remembers telling the Lewinskis he had used tissue expansion for numerous facial reconstructions of birth defects and deformities. Plastic surgery, he points out, is a field where accepted surgical procedures are commonly used to treat conditions that have not responded well to other approaches. He admits that he doesn't recall specifically saying point-blank to the Lewinskis that he never used tissue expansion in a situation exactly like this before; he didn't believe it was necessary, because it was ingrained in his explanation of his approach: He had utilized tissue expansion to treat facial deformities, and the Lewinskis knew their daughter had a rare condition, which had no common treatment. He considered the family's claim of ignorance to be less than sincere.

Mr. Gismondi disagreed. He continually reminded the jury that Dr. Hurwitz's approach was what the attorney considered unique. "I can't tell you the number of hours I spent searching the literature just to be able to accurately state one sentence in the courtroom, and that was to say either to him or to his expert, 'Isn't it true that there is not a single doctor in any textbook or medical article who has ever done this surgery for this condition, anywhere in the world?' That was the most powerful bit of evidence that I had."

Dr. Hurwitz and his attorney, like the judge, sensed they were in trouble. Mr. Gismondi, in Dr. Hurwitz's opinion, was very skilled at oversimplifying the case. In addition, Heather Lewinski gave teary-eyed testimony, and everyone in the courtroom, including Dr. Hurwitz, was sympathetic to her plight. The case seemed to take on an emotional tone rather than an analytical assessment of the validity of the treatment and informed consent. The time had come to offer a settlement, even though Dr. Hurwitz continued to believe he had done nothing wrong.

The offer reached seven figures. "It was not an insignificant amount of money, certainly by any stretch of the imagination," says Mr. Gismondi. "Although we never were presented with this scenario, I just have this feeling, in general—had that amount of money been offered three months earlier—six months earlier—whatever, before many psychological hurdles had been crossed, before the Lewinskis had actually been in the courtroom and seen things evolve, the chances of that money being accepted would have been greater."

Ms. Lewinski concurs. "Just from the mere fact of all Heather had been through, and not putting her through a trial, I think we would have settled before we arrived." But, in her mind, the offer came too late for her and her family. Their attorney didn't try to persuade them otherwise. "I was willing to roll the dice as well," he says.

After deliberating for 75 minutes following the weeklong trial, the 12 jurors reached a verdict. Dr. Hurwitz wouldn't be present when it was announced. He was scrubbing in for an operation. The Lewinskis, their attorney, and Dr. Hurwitz's attorney were all in the courtroom to hear the decision.

"That is a very emotional time," says Mr. Gismondi. As with any big case for a malpractice attorney, he says his heart was beating so hard it felt like it might jump out of his chest. "Anybody who says it's not is lying. There is nothing that a lawyer goes through that is more tense than watching that jury come back in the room, total silence in the room, having that verdict passed over to the clerk, you hear the paper unfolding, and hear that verdict read. There is nothing like it. It is a very tense time, and the announcement of the verdict leads to an immediate emotional reaction, though not always visibly. You are either elated or you are completely dejected."

Mr. Gismondi and his clients were elated. The jurors ordered Dr. Hurwitz to pay the Lewinskis $3.55 million for Heather's medical bills, the permanent disfigurement of her face, and her pain and suffering. The award was the largest amount in Allegheny County history and greatly exceeded Dr. Hurwitz's medical malpractice coverage.

Through all the elation, Mr. Gismondi had an interesting emotional reaction. He walked over to Dr. Hurwitz's attorney, Mr. Bass. "I remember saying to him, 'John, you tried a good case. I'm not out to hurt your guy.' He knew what that meant. I wasn't out to try to bankrupt him, put him out of business. That wasn't what it was about."

Ms. Lewinski wasn't quite so sympathetic. When the verdict was announced, there was great joy for her, her husband, and Heather, and also a tremendous relief and feeling of vindication. They also realized that the verdict had the potential to destroy Dr. Hurwitz from a professional standpoint and, perhaps, from a personal standpoint, too. But they had no feelings, for even just a moment, that the verdict went too far.

"Absolutely none!" Ms. Lewinski emphasizes. "I've heard since that his daughter was somehow murdered in the backyard. I cannot imagine any parent losing a child, ever. That, in itself, I feel sorry for him, based on the fact that happened to one of his kids." Her sympathy ends there. She reiterates that she had no misgivings about the size of the award and how it would affect his life and the life of his family.

Without a settlement, Dr. Hurwitz, once his insurance payout was confirmed, would be personally liable for as much as $2.5 million. Also, his malpractice insurance premium, now that he was a private practitioner, would no doubt skyrocket. But money was just one of his worries. News of the judgment was on the front page of the area's newspapers—the kind of publicity the private practitioner could ill afford.

From Dr. Hurwitz's standpoint it was all a great injustice. His crucial mistake in the case, in his mind, was his naiveté of the legal system.

"I didn't fully appreciate going up against a child with a facial deformity and a recognized outstanding malpractice attorney who could string information together in a damaging, not-quite-accurate, not-quite-deceitful manner. The conviction of my own performance kept me from recognizing the strength of the opposing forces in the context of a jury trial. I learned that there is much more to the making of a jury's verdict than medical decision making. The courts are a form of theater, of presentation.

"He [Mr. Gismondi] is a master. He was clever enough to know what to use, what not to use, how to work with the jury to keep it simple enough and clear enough, and where to focus. It didn't matter if was accurate or fair.

"He made me look like I was taking advantage of them [Heather and her family] when the opposite was the case; they were a family desperately looking for a solution, looking for help. They traveled to world centers about this. No one could come up with a plan. It should have been quite clear to them that it was an unusual situation, an unusual disease, and, necessarily, an unusual remedy.

"I was being punished for trying to be innovative and caring for her in the best way I knew. He [Mr. Gismondi] used my strength and made it a weakness. My strength was that I am an academic plastic surgeon, and I write papers, and when I write papers I subject my work to peer review. Very few doctors do that. I think that puts me in a special category of peer scrutiny. In his summation, he [Mr. Gismondi] says, 'Now I know what was on Dr. Hurwitz's mind; he was experimenting on this girl so that he could write another paper.' That was crafty because if the jury really, really believed what I did was not for her care, but for the purposes of writing a paper, then I should be guilty. But a scientific publication was never my intention. My oath as a physician is, first do no harm. But, he had the last word, and nobody could refute it. I will be forever wary of Mr. Gismondi for his cunning gamesmanship. And while I understand the dismay and anger of the Lewinskis, I fault the family for castigating me and rejecting my further care, while accepting multiple unsuccessful major operations by the Boston surgeons."

As soon as Dr. Hurwitz learned of the verdict, he contemplated an appeal. His lawyer, Mr. Bass, cited a number of possible legal transgressions that would be grounds for a retrial. But his client had grown tired of courtrooms. "I felt so beaten up and so emotionally distraught, I just wanted to move on," says Dr. Hurwitz. He worried that a retrial would have been disabling to Heather, also.

There would be no appeal, only some difficult lessons: "I had a humbling experience," he says. "I learned much from the court's adverse decision in my case. I failed to adequately respond to the anguish of the Lewinskis as Heather's scars contracted and displaced her lower lip. And I am ever the more diligent to inform patients of uncertain outcomes and alternative therapies, especially when considering innovative approaches."

Somehow, he had found the strength to salvage his life, his career, and his family when Karen was murdered. Just like his reaction to her murder, he vowed not to let this trial define him, no matter what the Lewinskis or the media thought. He knew the truth when it came to his care of Heather, and Linda knew the truth, and that was all that mattered to him.

After some lengthy negotiations, both sides came to a financial agreement. "We probably could have put him into bankruptcy, because he did not have enough insurance to cover that verdict," says Mr. Gismondi. His client decided not to do so.

"It wouldn't help anything," says Ms. Lewinski. That wasn't what I was looking to achieve. But do I feel sorry for the man? No."

"He did ultimately agree to pay a certain amount of money out of his own pocket, but it was certainly not enough to cover the verdict," adds Mr. Gismondi. The confidential payout was enough that, among other things that had to be sold, was the Seven Springs Mountain Resort condominium, which had been such a healing respite for the Hurwitzes that they had purchased it from their friends, the Rubins. Other fallout included Dennis's annual malpractice insurance premium, which more than tripled—from $60,000 to $200,000. His patient load also dipped.

His medical practice seemed to hang in the balance.

Although he says he remains respectful of the tort system's role in overseeing medical negligence, he can't help but be bitter at what the legal system allowed to happen. What particularly gnawed at him, what he feels permitted this to happen, was the testimony of Dr. John Mulliken, the plaintiff's expert witness. He was the doctor who first stated to Mr. Gismondi that Dr. Hurwitz's treatment of Heather was *not consistent with the standards of good practice*, which Mr. Gismondi acknowledged as the "critical moment" for pursuing the malpractice suit.

Dr. Hurwitz decided to write a letter to his colleague, with whom he was more than a casual acquaintance. Dr. Hurwitz says they admired each other's scientific writings. In fact, he recalls in the days just prior to Dr. Mulliken's adverse testimony, they had spent hours together in New York City discussing a newly published methodology of computer assessment of cleft lip repair, written by Dr. Hurwitz. It was that kind of professional rapport and respect that made Dr. Mulliken's role in the Lewinski case so exasperating to Dr. Hurwitz and that prompted his correspondence.

In the first page of the two-page typed letter, Dr. Hurwitz noted his efforts to diffuse the disappointment and anger of two Pittsburgh families who sustained significant complications from recent cleft-related surgery performed by Dr. Mulliken. Page two concerned the Lewinski case. After Dr. Hurwitz briefly reviewed his treatment for Heather, he described his thoughts of Dr. Mulliken's expert role:

I have thought about your damning testimony on a daily basis. Your condemnation made our convincing the jury of my good intentions and reasonable effort impossible. Your testimony was the critical factor that resulted in a plaintiff's jury award of over three million dollars, and that has brought me anguish, misery, and to the brink of personal and practice bankruptcy. If that were your intention, you have succeeded to nearly destroy a surgeon dedicated to the treatment of children. I can understand your disagreement of the use of a novel and creative form of treatment that had a significant complication, but to consider it outside of the standard of care for such a rare condition that you never personally examined and for which there are no published protocols is unreasonable and unforgivable. In fact, there are several publications in peer reviewed articles on a similar method of treatment for similar problems. Without supporting evidence, John Gismondi led the jury to believe that I was operating on Heather as an experiment in my eagerness to publish the results of another unique treatment. This perception of experimental surgery, which was supported by your testimony, was too much for the jurors to look past the fact that a reasonable and worthwhile approach was taken. Along with subsequent adverse reporting in the Pittsburgh Post-Gazette, that experience has brought me to the point of despair....

He closed the letter by making sure Dr. Mulliken understood the ramifications of his involvement.

Chapter Seventeen

I cannot understand your thoughtlessness, arrogance, and cruelty to me on academic, personal, and professional levels. You must be aware of the misery you have caused me and my family.

He never mailed the letter. One of his colleagues, Dr. Spear, talked him out of it by arguing that it would do nothing more than create further ill will. Not long afterward, though, Dr. Hurwitz and Dr. Mulliken attended the same medical meeting. It gave the defendant a chance to confront the expert witness. Dr. Hurwitz recalls the brief exchange:

"John, you know I lost the case."

"I heard. I feel terrible about that."

"You do?"

"What can I do to help you?"

"Give me a couple million dollars."

"What do you mean?"

"That is what I have left to pay, thanks to you."

"Oh, I didn't know it was that much."

"Yeah, it is."

"Well, I didn't mean helping like that. What else can I do?"

"You are no help."

They have not talked since, and Dr. Hurwitz has no plans to do so ever again.

"It should take an onerous, unforgiving action for a subsequent treating surgeon to say that the first doctor didn't follow the standard of care," says Dr. Hurwitz. "In hindsight, my judgment for treatment of this difficult case can be debated, but not whether it was malpractice. I used well-known techniques; I didn't invent the techniques. That is why I fought the case. I felt so right about the issues."

The confrontation didn't prompt Dr. Mulliken to retract his position. "I understand that for really good results sometimes you've got to be willing to operate near the precipice. But I'm not so sure in this case. It's all in my testimony."

It's testimony that Dr. Steven R. Buchman, a professor of plastic surgery at the University of Michigan, believes never should have taken place. He read Dr. Mulliken's *standards of good practice* letter when he was being considered as an expert defense witness for a possible appeal. His outrage rivals that of Dr. Hurwitz.

"Disingenuous," he says of the letter. "It's almost like you'd be thinking Dr. Hurwitz poured acid on somebody. It was like, 'Whoa, what were you thinking?! This is never done! You take somebody and put them in boiling water!' I thought the letter was well over the top. What Dr. Mulliken did was wrong."

He has no criticism of Dr. Hurwitz's original approach. "There is no great answer for that disease process," he explains. He can understand how someone who isn't a plastic surgeon, even Mr. Gismondi, might be confused by the use of tissue expanders as a treatment option. "It may be a little unusual, but where is the book that says this is the only way you reconstruct these really horrendous cases? I think, in a way, as plastic surgeons, we're dealing with being 'creative' all the time; we're trying to come up with creative solutions for problems that are not always textbook. It's not like you have a bad gallbladder, and it's there, and you take it out. You're talking about somebody's Romberg disease—it's not like she was normal to begin with. To me, Dennis shouldn't have lost."

Another strong supporter of Dr. Hurwitz is Dr. Ernest K. Manders, a Pittsburgh plastic surgeon who initiated a number of innovations in soft tissue expansion in the 1980s. Prior to coming to Pittsburgh, he was a professor of surgery and pediatrics, and chief of the Center for Soft Tissue expansion at Penn State, where he was succeeded by Dr. Mackay, who was the expert witness for Dr. Hurwitz.

"The malpractice suit was an absolute miscarriage of justice," he says bluntly. "I defy anyone to look at the facts of this case and conclude that Dennis Hurwitz is truly responsible for what happened."

He scoffs at Mr. Gismondi's contention that tissue expanders were never used for this condition.

"What the hell kind of argument is that? That is a total non-logical argument."

He gives an example. "I have on my leg a defect. It is a burn. I go to the literature; soft tissue expansion is used to replace burns. Now, I just come back from Africa and I have an envenomation from a black mamba's snakebite. I have this huge area of damaged skin. Now, if I go to the literature I probably can't find anything on that black mamba's snakebite or whatever because it is so rare, and I should be dead. So, now are you going to tell me I shouldn't have tissue expansion here, just like I might for a burn or shark bite or all those things that are already described in the literature? It is immaterial. You have a defect, you have skin around it, and tissue expansion is a logical thing to try. There is no better skin to reconstruct a defect than the skin immediately adjacent to it. That is the principle of plastic surgery. He did the perfectly logical thing. Many other people would have done the same thing."

Dr. Mackay agrees and wishes he had made that clear during his testimony. "The lawyer [Mr. Gismondi] kept saying to me are you aware of tissue expansion for this condition. I said, 'No.' I should have said, 'Yes.' Strictly, had it been used for the lower facial area, no. Has it been used for a variant, yes. The guy [Mr. Gismondi] just kept coming back and hammering me on it."

While it's conceivable that a poll of plastic surgeons might give some support for Dr. Mulliken's position, there is one plastic surgeon who most likely would not do so. The surgeon doesn't know Dr. Hurwitz personally, but he certainly knows the case. The surgeon is Dr. Breitbart, the same doctor who was the other expert witness on behalf of the plaintiff.

Dr. Breitbart says he originally formulated his conclusions based, in part, on his training with one of the pioneers in treating Romberg syndrome, Dr. John Siebert at New York University Medical Center. His experience there with Romberg and reconstruction was confined to microsurgical techniques to use filler material to restore the volume of the face rather than cutting out tissue and stitching it up "Maybe my experience with him made me biased in that sense," he admits.

Five years later, without reviewing the specifics of the case, Dr. Breitbart isn't prepared to retract everything he said at trial. "On the other hand," he says, "on a reflective look, you can make a case that it was not malpractice.

"In terms of whether malpractice was committed or not, I'm not sure. I would grant that, conceivably, if tissue expansion had been done under ideal circumstances, and you get optimal expansion, and all incisions are put in optimal places, and you get optimal healing, then, perhaps, you could get an optimal result."

Dr. Hurwitz is not reluctant to admit that the results were not optimal in the Lewinski case. But he also points out that a bad result is not bad medicine, which, oddly enough, is the same logic Mr. Gismondi uses in deciding whether a malpractice case has merit.

Dr. Breitbart concedes that the idea of using tissue expanders wasn't reckless. "I have no objection to innovative techniques and established techniques in some fields being applied to other applications. There is always a first in any procedure, and, sometimes, it turns out being the dominant treatment."

One of the key questions raised in the trial, pertaining to the innovative treatment, was whether the Lewinskis gave informed consent. "I think that it is always a difficult case to prove," says Dr. Breitbart. "It's hard to support lack of informed consent, because Dr. Hurwitz probably explained to the patient the general kinds of complications of tissue expansion."

What particularly bothers Dr. Breitbart is how Dr. Hurwitz is portrayed in the eyes of the Lewinski family:

"Once Dr. Hurwitz did his surgery, I guess, in the view of the family, he was portrayed as the bad guy, and for any other surgeries that were done to try and change things, those surgeons were portrayed as the good guys, even if those surgeries would ultimately give her a result that is not pleasing and, potentially, even less pleasing than if she would have continued with the tissue expansion type procedures."

Blaming Dr. Hurwitz for Heather Lewinski's appearance is, says Dr. Breitbart, an oversimplified, unjust view of the case: "He meant no harm. He was a surgeon who was looking for a great result. I don't have any doubts about that. In a case like this, it is kind of hard to say if she would have had, say a free flap operation, how normal she would have looked."

Her six subsequent surgeries in Boston, outside of Dr. Hurwitz's care, only further cloud the issue in Dr. Breitbart's opinion: "Once she starts to have all those surgeries, it's hard to know how those kinds of surgeries can potentially contribute to an ultimate, unfavorable appearance."

These post-trial observations by Dr. Breitbart and his self-doubt about his testimony began to take root not long after the trial ended. He realized he owed something to Dr. Hurwitz. Five years later, he paid that self-imposed debt.   "I've been meaning to do it for years," he says.

Dr. Hurwitz had no idea what was about to take place. "He came up to me in a meeting in Orlando, the two of us were relatively isolated, sort of away from people," says Dr. Hurwitz. "I didn't even recognize him; I couldn't even place who he was." But after Dr. Breitbart introduced himself, he would remember the following conversation.

"I just want to tell you," Dr. Breitbart told him, "that I did the wrong thing. I shouldn't have testified against you, and I regret it. You should know that. I just don't want you to hold it against me."

"Well, you should understand it was a very painful experience," a startled Dr. Hurwitz replied. "I don't think I deserved to lose the case. I'll never get over it personally, emotionally, and financially." Silence then ensued. Evidently, Dr. Breitbart had nothing left to say. Dennis finally uttered what he imagined his colleague hoped to hear.

"If you're asking for my forgiveness, I accept your apology; I won't hold it against you or let it color my feelings about you."

With that, the conversation ended.

"I was stunned, speechless. Why would he apologize after all these years?" wonders Dr. Hurwitz. "I didn't ask him what he really meant by it. Was it because he shouldn't have treated me that way? Was it because the case wasn't valid enough? He obviously was seeking my absolution, because he was really troubled by his actions. I don't have this intense desire to explore it further. He did the wrong thing, he told me he did the wrong thing, and he doesn't want this to come between us. I just hope he is more cautious if this kind of situation comes up again."

It appears Dr. Breitbart—now in private practice with offices in Manhattan and Long Island—did indeed gain a new perspective. "In this particular case, if I had to do it over again, I wouldn't get involved. I think Dr. Hurwitz is a good surgeon; I've referred patients to him."

The Lewinskis, though, will never agree with Dr. Breitbart's revised assessment of Dr. Hurwitz. To her credit, Heather's search of beauty has gone beyond her appearance. She graduated from high school and enrolled in college, majoring in education. "She is doing very well," says her mom. "She's adjusted well. Given the cards she was dealt, I think she is doing very well."

She says, though, that she and Heather remain angry at Dr. Hurwitz. "If at some point he would have contacted us, that would have changed my opinion of him. If at some point during the trial he would have acted differently, that would have changed my opinion of him. If at some point after the trial we got some sort of letter from him, that would have changed my opinion of him. But none of that ever happened. So, what is there to say now? It's much too late. I do not believe that Dr. Hurwitz ever took the time, or had the inclination, to think about how this changed Heather's life. I don't mean to sound dramatic—he lost a child. I didn't lose a child physically, but certain aspects of her childhood, we lost. Certain aspects of her adulthood, she will never have. So therefore, he took something from us that wasn't his to take. And I don't think he realizes that—the impact it had on my marriage, he will never understand, the impact it had on us financially—he will never understand."

Linda actually mentioned to her husband that he should write a letter, but not a letter of apology or seeking forgiveness. When her husband replied that he didn't see the point of sending something that would only inflame the Lewinskis' loathing of him, Linda decided to start writing her own letter to Ms. Lewinski. It was hand written in pen, on two pieces of paper torn out of a notebook:

Mrs. Lewinski,

God and nature gave your child her deformity, but instead of accepting fate and helping your lovely daughter accept who she was and focus on living with her problem, you went in search of a cure. You begged the doctor to help. You knew this was so rare; thus you knew he could not have done the exact procedure on other patients. But you wanted him to try and change fate. You are mad at yourself for putting your daughter through all that anyway. You are raging at God for doing this to you, but since you couldn't sue God, you sued the doctor to satisfy your cry for justice and to scapegoat your guilt onto someone else....

Dennis didn't need to read any further. He told his wife not to bother finishing the letter. It should not be sent. Just like in his un-mailed letter to Dr. Mulliken, the world of medicine had merely become a backdrop for spewing more animosity, more divisiveness, more blame. Dr. Hurwitz was a doctor, not an attorney, not an orator, not a jury. He wanted to heal people, nothing more. Linda would not send the letter, nor would he write one to Ms. Lewinsky or to Heather.

When Mr. Gismondi paraded Heather before Congress in February 2003 to testify against President George W. Bush's tort reform proposal that would limit medical malpractice awards to $250,000, Dr. Hurwitz kept silent. When Heather was featured in a June 2003 *People* magazine article about her surgeries and the lawsuit, he chose again not to directly respond to the media or to the family.

"It made no sense to me, appealing to her [Ms. Lewinski's] sensitivities; she feels the courts have vindicated everything she and her family thought about me. They won, and they think I should be gracious and say, 'I was wrong all the way.' While I sympathize with the Pittsburgh and Boston medical ordeal they have been through, I don't feel that I have wronged them."

There were others who questioned Dr. Hurwitz. But not about the Lewinski case. The front-page headline in the newspaper provided Mr. Gismondi with some priceless free advertising for his services. He says he fielded some calls from people who wanted to file malpractice suits against Dr. Hurwitz. "I sort of attributed that to people reading the newspaper," he says. "They see their opportunity."

Just like he did with the Lewinski case, he did his research on each of the claims to see if any of the cases had merit. "I never took one of them," he says.

The Chase for Beauty

Chapter Eighteen

D r. Hurwitz doesn't deny that the Lewinski case could have destroyed his medical career and his personal life. He realized it was imperative to create a plan of action just like he had done so many times before—after the University of Pittsburgh unexpectedly slashed his salary by one-third; after the same university surprisingly withdrew support for his professional dream, the Aesthetic Plastic Surgery Center; after he faced the grim prospect that his daughter's murderer could walk away a free man at the conclusion of the retrial; after finding the unimaginable, his daughter brutally murdered in his backyard; after the young woman he fell in love with at first sight broke his heart by choosing not to be his girlfriend.

"Frankly, it could have crushed me," he says of the Lewinski verdict. So could any of the other setbacks, but he had persevered. Yet, that gave him no solace. "I was really worried. I had no money, and I couldn't borrow because there was a judgment against me. It is like bad credit. I was distressed."

He thought like a surgeon. The plan was simple. Decisive. He needed patients, and he needed to restore his credibility. Relying on referrals from his satisfied patients wouldn't be enough. What he didn't need to do was bolster his confidence. "The verdict shook me, but it never made me lose faith in my skills as a surgeon." Fortunately for him, his physician colleagues hadn't lost faith in him, either. Dr. Schauer, who directed the bariatric weight loss surgery team at the University of Pittsburgh, continued to recommend Dr. Hurwitz to his formerly obese patients whose weight loss had caused excess skin issues.

His growing number of body contouring operations formed the foundation of his planned resurgence. The surge in popularity of bariatric surgery meant there would be a corresponding surge in body contouring patients; and, just as important, he was extraordinarily consistent at getting excellent results with his influx of patients.

One of his success stories was Laura Smolenak. After a lifelong battle of losing and then gaining weight, she had gastric bypass by Dr. Schauer in October 1998. By then, she tipped the scale at more than 300 pounds. About 18 months later, she had lost 162 pounds. But she wasn't happy. "I had serious skin issues," she says. "I finally overcame this tragedy of obesity, but I was left with this sad-looking body. I just felt so uncomfortable as a human being; I just felt nonsexual."

It was health issues, related to obesity—including back pain and severe hypertension that threatened her kidney function—that prompted Laura to have the bypass surgery in the first place. She didn't give much thought to the cosmetic outcome and had no idea that rolls of stretched skin on the arms, the thighs, the stomach, were a potential outcome from significant weight loss. "I was kind of clueless," says Laura, who was an intensive care nurse.

She found the reality of living with excess skin to be very depressing. Dr. Schauer recommended she make an appointment with Dr. Hurwitz. They met in the fall of 1999. It was not an easy consultation for Laura. "I was so embarrassed—to be a woman and to stand stark naked in front of a man with skin issues. I just thought I would die," she says. She felt great relief when Dr. Hurwitz didn't recoil at the sight of what she considered a body deformity. Instead, Dr. Hurwitz devised a plan. They established a goal weight that she needed to reach before body-contouring surgery was practical. "Dr. Hurwitz just made me feel like he could make me whole again. He won me over."

In February 2000, she reached her ideal weight range, around 140 pounds. Her body contouring could begin. "I decided to have my surgeries done in two stages. One was to have my arms done, and I needed some work on my head—I had two chins. I had a lot of skin in my neck, and my eyebrows hung over my eyes, and I thought I needed to have my eyes lifted, but Dr. Hurwitz told me, 'No.' It was that I lost the fat in my head, and my forehead sank. He needed to do a brow lift."

The results, she says, were spectacular. "I didn't have to duct tape the skin under my arms anymore, and I looked 10 years younger."

Contouring of the lower body followed two months later. "I needed a full lower-body contour, because I was a bottom-heavy girl, kind of like the Queen song, 'fat-bottomed girls make the world girl round,' that was me." There was significant swelling after that procedure. "My legs were like trees for a year," she says. It turned out she had unusually prolonged swelling in her legs called lymphedema.

"I wore a long skirt or pants every day." But she never lost faith in Dr. Hurwitz. "He would say, 'Give this three months,' and 'Give this six months,' whatever, and that is what happened. Everything Dr. Hurwitz told me came true. He changed my life. He made me feel whole as a woman and gave me back my sexuality. His work is like fine art. The Lord had definitely gifted the man, because after he was done, I would never ever have dreamed that I would wear a bikini, and it came to be. My plastic surgery is what really changed my life psychosocially. It really did. I have referred a lot of business to him, because I believe in him," says Laura, who became the patient care coordinator for Dr Schauer's practice. "I'm so proud of the work Dr. Hurwitz has done. I show my body to other women, and I can see in their eyes that they have lost all hope to feel whole again, and I know how that feels and to show them my body, they are just like, 'Wow!' It gives them faith, too—to finish losing the weight and believe they can be whole again, to feel sexual as a woman again. The plastic surgery is really what I needed to be whole again," she says. "It was a gift. Dr. Hurwitz has really enriched my life. I want to go dance again."

It wasn't just the patients who were impressed with Dr. Hurwitz's results. One of his residents in training commented that his teacher's surgical results were exceptional. "Why do you keep it a secret?" he asked Dr. Hurwitz. "You should get the stories of your successful patients on television and newspapers," he advised. "Nobody gets the quality results you do."

Chapter Eighteen

The Lewinski verdict, with its front-page negative headlines, certainly made Dr. Hurwitz receptive to creating an upscale, positive public image. "I needed to get my name out there," he says. So, he took his resident's offhand comment to heart and incorporated it into his revival plan. He began a multimedia campaign to let the world know, not just plastic surgeons and his patients, the success he was having in the operating room. He hired a Manhattan public relations firm experienced in the beauty market on a national scale. He contracted a medical self-publishing firm to write his book on body contouring. He gave scientific lectures to plastic surgeons and experiential lectures to the public. He prepared submissions for magazines and prestigious scientific journals, which were regularly published. A California-based medical Web site company developed for him sophisticated and informative domains with effective search engine optimization. Soon, his clinical excellence was apparent everywhere on the Internet. He also appeared on television shows—local and nationally syndicated programs, including special stories on Discovery Health Channel.

In the court of public opinion, his marketing efforts had helped restore both his credibility and desirability. A multitude of new patients for a broad spectrum of procedures made that very clear. But Dr. Hurwitz didn't want to settle for just being considered an accomplished plastic surgeon. When he walked through the halls at medical meetings, in hospitals, he wanted—always wanted—plastic surgeons to recognize him for his clinical contributions. So, he directed his work ethic, his creative thinking toward body contouring, because the rapidly growing in-demand operation didn't have a modus operandi among surgeons. And for good reason. It wasn't an easy procedure, not for the doctor and not for the patient. After her upper body lift, Laura says, "I felt like someone who had been hit by a train." Waking up after her lower body lift had been completed was no better: "I was so overwhelmed with so much discomfort. I was cut from my ankles to my groin. He fixed me like I was 18 again, took all the stretch marks out of my lower abdomen, made me a new belly button, pulled the skin up from my knees up like a pair of pants, tucked in my butt, took a diamond of skin out of my back and my waist. I probably had about 12 feet of incisions all at one time. That is big. I had a catheter in, because I couldn't even walk to the bathroom to go pee. I was totally dependent on someone for several days."

It concerned Dr. Hurwitz that he had to repeatedly put his patients through so much pain after each stage of body contouring. In part, it led him to thinking that he could perform a lower body lift and an upper body lift at the same time, what he would call a single-stage Total Body Lift.

His signature operation was born. "Patients don't want a half-dozen smaller operations unless they are having troubles," he says. "My analogy is, 'Do you want a nonstop transcontinental flight to Los Angeles, or do you want to take four short halls to get there?' Every time you fly there is a risk of going up and down. Well, every time you have surgery, you assume new risks of anesthesia and surgical complications."

He actually did his first single-stage Total Body Lift, before it had a proper name, in February 2001. Both he and his patient were pleased with the result.

Dr. Hurwitz officially introduced the Total Body Lift as a single-stage body contouring procedure at the 2003 Northeastern Society of Plastic Surgeons' annual meeting in Baltimore. The term came to him as he was writing his scientific paper for the meeting. He advocated consideration of the single-stage procedure for problems of loose skin from the shoulders to the knees, including the breasts, arms, abdomen, hips, back, buttocks, and thighs.

He explained that Total Body Lift surgery begins with the patient lying on his or her stomach while he removes excess skin from above the buttocks to the mid-back and along the back of the thighs, which tightens the lower body. Cuts are made along the waistline and the inside of the thigh. Then, the patient is turned onto his or her back while still under anesthesia, and Dr. Hurwitz then removes more skin from the stomach, the front of the thighs, and under the arms. For women, he then redistributes a flap of skin from the upper back by rebuilding the breast using that excess skin rather than an implant. A new belly button is created and remaining skin is contoured. Scars are hidden, wherever possible, in the skin's natural folds or in inconspicuous places that typically would be hidden by underwear. He estimated that, depending on the size of the patient and skill and number of his assistants, the Total Body Lift should take seven to 13 hours to complete, remove 10 to 30 pounds of excess skin, and take about six weeks recovery time for the patient.

There has been no public criticism from his peers, says Dr. Hurwitz, though he imagines there is an ongoing undercurrent of wariness. "I think the main reason I'm not invited to some of the national meetings panels or be a keynote speaker at medical meetings is that there is concern among some plastic surgeons that the Total Body Lift is too ambitious for one procedure despite the benefits to the patient. People have told me at meetings that some hierarchies say that they are worried that those who do it are not capable of doing it. They're saying, 'Hurwitz can do it, but we don't recommend it.' But I haven't had a written criticism of it." Not from his peers, not from his patients, and not from Dr. Pories, one of the founders of bariatric surgery who wrote the glowing foreword to Dr. Hurwitz's book, *Total Body Lift*.

Dr. Hurwitz says it's understandable for a general plastic surgeons to have reservations about single-stage Total Body Lift surgery. Spending as many as 13 hours in an operating room with one patient can be physically and mentally draining. Yet, it's where he seems most at home. For each operation, he assembles an OR team—an associate plastic surgeon trained by him, nurses, medical technicians, an anesthesiologist, a physician's assistant, a plastic surgery resident, and medical students. He is the sculptor, or so it seems, during patient preparation, where he spends up to an hour making comprehensive and exacting preoperative markings directly on the patient's skin. Once the surgery begins, the team chatters like they are gathered around a water cooler, not a patient on an operating table. Dr. Hurwitz is just one of the gang. But, at times, there is complete silence while he performs an intricate surgical maneuver or searches for an obstinate bleeder. Every incision he makes is without hesitation. He is bold, confident in his hands, always thinking ahead. He works quickly but is never in a hurry. He calmly and thoroughly answers every question by his surgical team. Sometimes, he provides answers to unasked questions. It's as if he wants to share his invigorating experience with whoever wants to listen. Any moments of tension as the hours pass are overridden by his serenity. Like a conductor, he oversees each member of his surgical team. He constantly positions and repositions the members for efficiency and effectiveness of the tasks. If an assistant's stitches are imprecise, Dr. Hurwitz has the work redone. He is the maestro, the OR is his stage, and the patient is his symphony. Even though he is on his feet, hour after hour, often with only some peanut butter crackers and a cup of tea for nourishment, he continues to be fresh, alert, alive. He is in his element, a universe that he controls. The rest of the world must wait outside.

The Total Body Lift not only invigorates Dr. Hurwitz, it evidently invigorates those around him. In 2005, the University of Pittsburgh plastic surgery residents voted him Teacher of the Year, an honor typically bestowed upon full-time professors, not part-time associate professors like Dr. Hurwitz.

The media across the country has taken notice, too. Dr. Hurwitz has become a sought-after expert, which he thoroughly embraces. "I realize the originality and the value of the Total Body Lift and the need to make it known and understood to both plastic surgeons and the public." Most advances in medicine have a much more traditional route. "The usual process is laborious—presentations and meetings, publications of papers, recognition by plastic surgeons, and, ultimately, the public sort of finds out indirectly, through the grapevine of plastic surgeons," says Dr. Hurwitz. It's the kind of approach— the only approach—that has the approval of Dr. McWilliams, one of Dr. Hurwitz's mentors, who abhors doctors in the media spotlight. While Dr. Hurwitz has followed that traditional scientific presentation approach, the Lewinski verdict made him receptive to making the public aware of his Total Body Lift breakthrough, including the writing of *Total Body Lift*, which he freely admits is written for both doctors and patients.

Chapter Eighteen

The Total Body Lift surgery helped rescue his medical practice; it didn't rescue his marriage. His marriage didn't need to be saved. The Hurwitzes' passion for each other could not be doused by the world around them—not in public, not in the courtroom, not in their home, and not in their bedroom. Their love for each other, they say, begins with respect for each other.

"I am proud of Linda, of her accomplishments, and her caring spirit," says her husband. "We emphasize the other's attributes and minimize each others shortcomings. The major bond," he adds, "is our satisfying sexual relationship. While my love is still beautiful, and sensual, it is her enraptured spirit that is most captivating. And I'll be damned if I was going to let my own financial worries from the Lewinski verdict—we were destitute—get in the way of our physical relationship, just like I wasn't going to let Karen's death upset our bedroom. The bedroom has a certain life of its own, and if the troubles of your life intrude in there, then the marriage is over."

They survived the Lewinski saga the same way they survived Karen's murder—together. And four years after the Lewinski verdict, the loyal, supportive, loving wife and the renowned plastic surgeon would attend together the dinner in Chicago honoring Dr. Spear as the outgoing president of the American Society of Plastic Surgeons. Life had moved forward again for Dr. Hurwitz.

He and his wife sat, at their table of 10, with other plastic surgeons and their wives, most of them casual acquaintances from years of plastic surgery meetings across the country. Talk invariably revolved around shopping, golf, restaurants, the weather, and other dinner-party chatter. In the midst of the music, the clanging of silverware, and the pockets of conversation, one of the doctors at the Hurwitzes' table leaned over to say something to both of them. "I have to tell you how badly I feel about your daughter; I can't forget what happened."

It had been nearly 16 years since October 27, 1989. In that time, the Hurwitzes had started a new family, continued with their careers, endured misfortune, celebrated triumphs, and, ultimately, chose to not live in despair; yet it was Karen's death, not even her life, that was still so much a part of them to strangers, to acquaintances, to friends, to family, even to themselves.

"I still cry," says Dr. Hurwitz. His wife says she does, too. "I'll be going along fine and something, anything, will trigger it, and I just start crying."

Karen's death also remains an integral part of Michale Anderson's life. Incarcerated for the rest of his life in a state penitentiary about 60 miles south of Pittsburgh, he says he has reconciled himself to what he calls a "lifetime of pain." Despite the passage of time, he has no great message, nothing to add about what happened that fateful night—even though in his statement at the end of the original trial he intimated he would one day have an explanation for his actions.

"I miss Karen," he simply says. Through all the years, she has never once come to him in a dream to say goodbye, as she did with her parents. While Mick has had no spiritual closure with Karen, he offers all he can at this point to her parents. "I am so very sorry that I killed their daughter. I blame no one but me for the ultimate act of killing."

The apology means nothing to the man who lost a daughter. "What has come to light after all these years? Nothing. He is just a thug. This man must never be out on the streets."

The Chicago dinner-gala revelation by the acquaintance at the Hurwitzes' table didn't ruin the evening for either of them. They have learned not to wallow in self-pity. "I always grapple between my misery of not having her here and her misery of losing her own life," says Dr. Hurwitz. "When I feel sorry for myself—like when I hear a song that she liked and I really, really miss her—I sort of snap to and remember that my pain doesn't compare to her pain, the metaphysical pain of not existing. She's not here. I am."

Chapter Eighteen

So are Jeffrey and Julia. "We were able to adopt these two amazing kids," says Linda. "They helped us heal, gave us a family again, gave us the joy of experiencing their childhoods." Her husband couldn't agree more. Jeffrey and Julia gave them love, continue to give them love, and let their parents love them. "I don't know if we would have survived without them," their father says.

Less than a month after the Chicago meeting, the Dr. Hurwitz road show continued. This time the stop was New York City, with family in tow, for a segment on NBC's *Today*, the number one morning show in the United States. On Thursday, October 20, 2005, at 8:12 AM, the segment began:

Matt Lauer (studio profile):

Imagine, finally losing a lot of weight and having something close to the body you've always wanted, only to find that you're still literally uncomfortable in your own skin. Dramatic weight loss from gastric bypass surgery can leave behind loads of leftover skin, a new and embarrassing reminder of your old body. Well, a procedure called a Total Body Lift removes that excess skin in one extensive surgery. Recently, we followed someone who tried it.

Matt Lauer (voiceover while a montage of patient Melissa Janci is shown):

Melissa Janci's weight gain began in college; after trying everything to trim down, she decided to take a dramatic step: gastric bypass surgery. Melissa lost 120 pounds, went from size 26 to a size four, and felt like a new woman.

Melissa Janci (taped):

Physically, I could do a lot more. I could exercise; I could walk without getting out of breath.

212

The Chase for Beauty

Matt Lauer (voiceover):

But the transformation that should have given Melissa self-confidence and a new lease on life instead left her self-conscious with a new problem.

Melissa Janci (taped):

Though you lose weight, you have a lot of extra skin that kind of hangs.

Matt Lauer (voiceover):

Melissa decided to see Dr. Dennis Hurwitz, one of the few plastic surgeons who performs a Total Body Lift, to tuck and snip away unwanted skin all over the body.

Dr. Hurwitz (taped in office):

They have to be healthy and lost most of the weight they need to lose and highly motivated.

Matt Lauer (voiceover):

The surgery can take hours. Patients get three layers of stitches, risk infections and blood clots, and face up to two months of recuperation. Melissa says for her the benefits far outweighed the risks.

Melissa Janci (taped):

To just stand up straighter and be more confident, I just felt it will help me all around.

[live shot showing Melissa Janci and Patricia Schneider.]

Chapter Eighteen

Matt Lauer:

Melissa Janci had that surgery two weeks ago. Patricia Schneider had her Total Body Lift a year ago. [shot of Dr. Hurwitz] Dr. Dennis Hurwitz is their plastic surgeon and author of [shot of book] the Total Body Lift. *Good morning to all of you.*

[live shot of all]

Group:

Morning, morning.

Matt Lauer:

[Melissa] how are you feeling, first of all?

Melissa Janci:

I feel good, actually.

Matt Lauer:

Two weeks after this extensive surgery, soreness? What about numbness, anything like that?

Melissa Janci:

The first couple days were bad, were rough, I have to admit that.

Matt Lauer:

When did you turn the corner?

The Chase for Beauty

Melissa Janci:

After, I'd say, the first three days, when I could get up out of bed, walk around, and start to feel a lot better.

Matt Lauer:

We saw some footage and, by the way, I think you were very brave to allow us to shoot that footage—

Melissa Janci:

Thanks!

Matt Lauer:

—what were the areas of the body in terms of excess skin that bothered you the most?

Melissa Janci:

Definitely the stomach area.

Matt Lauer:

Right in your stomach, arms?

Melissa Janci:

Yeah, arms, definitely, you have the flabby patch under your arms; legs, you have that little saddle bag on the side, and it's all gone now.

Matt Lauer:

Doctor, I know you were happy with the way Melissa did in surgery. How is she doing in recovery?

Chapter Eighteen

Dr. Hurwitz:

She's exceptional, truly a courageous young woman to come here and talk to you and talk to us about her experience. The operation took about seven hours, and we were able to do everything from her breasts down to her thighs.

Matt Lauer:

I was reading about this, and the first question that came to mind is why one long surgery, and why not do this piecemeal over a longer period of time?

Dr. Hurwitz:

It's possible to do it piecemeal, and, at times, we do, but for smaller, younger, energetic patients, we can do it all at once, because I have a team of surgeons working with me, an excellent hospital, at Magee-Womens Hospital in Pittsburgh, so we can do it.

Matt Lauer:

[Melissa], you lost about 120 pounds after gastric bypass surgery. Trish, you lost about 160, 165 pounds?

Patricia Schneider:
Correct.

Matt Lauer:

How discouraging was it for you? When you lost all that weight, you thought, "Okay, it's the new me." And you looked in the mirror and saw all this old skin?

The Chase for Beauty

Patricia Schneider:

It's terrible. You go though this whole process, and I never even considered doing that before, you get to a point where you lose all this weight, and then what you're left with is a little disappointing. You have extra skin; you can't fit in your clothing, you know, so you decide you have to do something about it.

Matt Lauer:

So, you had this body lift a year ago. When you look at yourself naked now, how does your opinion of what you see changed, or how has it changed compared to what you saw a year ago?

Patricia Schneider:

It's a hundred percent different.

Matt Lauer:

You feel the transformation from the heavier you, 160 pounds ago to now, is complete?

Patricia Schneider:

I do. I'm perfectly happy with the way I am. It's an amazing difference from the sizes I went down just from the, after the body lift, to now. It's amazing.

Matt Lauer:

What about the scarring. You know when you do this many surgeries over the, you know, size of a body, where do you hide these scars?

Chapter Eighteen

Dr. Hurwitz:

It's very important to make the scars as inconspicuous as possible—

Matt Lauer:

Because that can affect their body image also if they look in the mirror?

Dr. Hurwitz:

No question about it, so we try to hide them in the bikini line, hide them for women in the brassiere line, and creep them under the arms.

Matt Lauer:

Gastric bypass surgery can be pricy. Add to that now the cost of this Total Body Lift, which is about what?

Dr. Hurwitz:

That runs somewhere between 40 and 50 thousand dollars to get this completely done.

Matt Lauer:

So, it's important to tell patients who are lining up for gastric bypass surgery that they may want to consider this cost on top of that, if they really want to be in an emotional place after these surgeries where they want to be.

Melissa Janci:

When you're having the gastric bypass, all you think is, "I just want to lose the weight! I just want to lose the weight!" You don't realize you

The Chase for Beauty

lost the weight, and now you're still feeling uncomfortable, and this is the choice—

Patricia Schneider:

I was warned. They did tell you, but you put that out of your mind, and you're saying, "One step at a time." You know I wasn't thinking, "Oh, you know I have to go get plastic surgery after this." It wasn't even a consideration. They did warn you, but you decide that you got to take care of one thing at a time.

Matt Lauer:

I'll end with you Melissa. You're two weeks out of surgery, so you can see some of the results right now. Very encouraged by what you're seeing?

Melissa Janci:

Oh, yeah! [giggle] Yeah, I can't wait until it's all healed and better. It's been great.

Matt Lauer:

Well, good luck to you; Melissa, thanks. Trish, thank you very much; and Doctor, thank you as well.

Dr. Hurwitz:
Your welcome, Matt.

Matt Lauer:
And, we're back in a moment; this is Today on NBC.

Chapter Eighteen

With those concluding words, the five-minute segment ended. Dr. Hurwitz was pleased. So were his patients. So were the *Today* show producers. After a family picture with Matt Lauer and some shopping in Manhattan, the Hurwitzes returned home to Pittsburgh. For Dr. Hurwitz, that meant more patients. More interviews. More scientific papers. More invited lectures. More praise. More criticism. More nights out with his wife. More games of catch with the kids in the backyard. More golf. More skiing. More life to live.

None of it, he realizes—the achievements, the setbacks, the comebacks, the love—will ever make him forget about what happened to Karen. More than anything else, it is her incomprehensible fate that her father quietly says will forever define his life: "I look at myself like damaged goods. I'll never be quite the same."

That may be true, but for all his training and experience in making people look more attractive, the renowned plastic surgeon may not fully comprehend that, amid imperfection, beauty can miraculously emerge.

Printed in the USA
CPSIA information can be obtained
at www.ICGtesting.com
JSHW082200140824
68134JS00014B/348